DATE DUE

PRINTED IN U.S.A.

GOVERNMENT INTELLIGENCE AGENCIES

CRIME AND DETECTION

GOVERNMENT INTELLIGENCE AGENCIES

Joanna Rabiger

Foreword by Manny Gomez, Esq.

MASON CREST

Mason Crest
450 Parkway Drive, Suite D
Broomall, PA 19008
www.masoncrest.com

First printing
9 8 7 6 5 4 3 2 1

Series ISBN: 978-1-4222-3469-3
Hardcover ISBN: 978-1-4222-3478-5
ebook ISBN: 978-1-4222-8405-6

Library of Congress Cataloging-in-Publication Data on file with the Library of Congress

Developed and Produced by Print Matters Productions, Inc. (www.printmattersinc .com)

Developmental Editor: Amy Hackney Blackwell
Cover and Interior Design: Tom Carling, Carling Design Inc.

Note on Statistics: While every effort has been made to provide the most up-to-date government statistics, the Department of Justice and other agencies compile new data at varying intervals, sometimes as much as ten years. Agency publications are often based on data compiled from a period ending a year or two before the publication date.

CONTENTS

KEY ICONS TO LOOK FOR:

Text-Dependent Questions: These questions send the reader back to the text for more careful attention to the evidence presented there.

Words to Understand: These words with their easy-to-understand definitions will increase the reader's understanding of the text while building vocabulary skills.

Series Glossary of Key Terms: This back-of-the-book glossary contains terminology used throughout this series. Words found here increase the reader's ability to read and comprehend higher-level books and articles in this field.

Research Projects: Readers are pointed toward areas of further inquiry connected to each chapter. Suggestions are provided for projects that encourage deeper research and analysis.

Sidebars: This boxed material within the main text allows readers to build knowledge, gain insights, explore possibilities, and broaden their perspectives by weaving together additional information to provide realistic and holistic perspectives.

FOREWORD

Experience Counts

Detecting crime and catching lawbreakers is a very human endeavor. Even the best technology has to be guided by human intelligence to be used effectively. If there's one truth from my thirty years in law enforcement and security, it's trust your gut.

When I started on the police force, I learned from older officers and from experience what things to look for, what traits, characteristics, or indicators lead to somebody who is about to commit a crime or in the process of committing one. You learn from experience. The older generation of law enforcement teaches the younger generation, and then, if you're good, you pick up your own little nuances as to what bad guys are doing.

In my early work, I specialized in human intelligence, getting informants to tell me what was happening on the street. Most of the time it was people I arrested that I then "flipped" to inform me where the narcotics were being stored, how they were being delivered, how they were being sold, the patterns, and other crucial details.

A good investigator has to be organized since evidence must be presented in a legally correct way to hold up in court. Evidence from a crime scene has to have a perfect chain of custody. Any mishandling turns the evidence to fruits of a poisonous tree.

At my company, MG Security Services, which provides private security to corporate and individual clients in the New York area, we are always trying to learn and to pass on that learning to our security officers in the field.

Certainly, the field of detection has evolved dramatically in the last 100 years. Recording devices have been around for a long time; it's just that now they've gotten really good. Today, a pen can be a video recording device; whereas in the old days it would have been a large box with two wheels. The equipment was awkward and not too subtle: it would be eighty degrees out, you'd be sweating in a raincoat, and the box would start clicking.

The forensic part of detection is very high-tech these days, especially with DNA coming into play in the last couple of decades. A hundred years ago, fingerprinting revolutionized detective work; the next breakthrough is facial recognition. We have recently discovered that the arrangement of facial features (measured as nodes) is unique to each individual. No two people on the planet have the exact same configuration of nodes. Just as it took decades to build out the database of known fingerprints, facial recognition is a work in progress. We will see increasing collection of facial data when people obtain official identification. There are privacy concerns, but we're working them out. Facial recognition will be a centerpiece of future detection and prevention efforts.

Technology offers law enforcement important tools that we're learning to apply strategically. Algorithms already exist that allow retailers to signal authorities when someone makes a suspicious purchase—known bomb-making ingredients, for example. Cities are loaded with sensors to detect the slightest trace of nuclear, biological, or chemical materials that pose a threat to the public. And equipment nested on streetlights in New York City can triangulate the exact block where a gun was fired.

Now none of this does anything constructive without well-trained professionals ready and able to put the information to use. The tools evolve, but what doesn't evolve is human intelligence.

Law enforcement as a community is way ahead in fighting street and violent crime than the newer challenges of cybercrime and terrorism. Technology helps, but it all goes back to human intelligence. There is no substitute for the cop on the street, knowing what is going on in the neighborhood, knowing who the players are. When the cop has quality informants inside gangs, he or she knows when there's going to be a hit, a drug drop, or an illicit transaction. The human intelligence comes first; then you can introduce the technology, such as hidden cameras or other surveillance.

The twin challenges for domestic law enforcement are gangs and guns. Gangs are a big problem in this country. That's a cultural and social phenomenon that law enforcement has not yet found an effective way to counteract. We need to study that more diligently. If we're successful in getting rid of the gangs, or at least diluting them, we will have come a long way in fighting violent crime. But guns are the main issue. You look at England, a first-world country of highly educated people that strictly regulates guns, and the murder rate is minimal.

When it comes to cybercrime, we're woefully behind. That's simply because we hire people for the long term, and their skills get old. You have a twenty-five-year-old who's white-hot now, but guess what? In five years that skill set is lost. Hackers, on the other hand, are young people who tend to evolve fast. They learn so much more than their older law-enforcement counterparts and are able to penetrate systems too easily. The Internet was not built with the security of private users in mind. It is like a house with no door locks, and now we're trying to figure ways to secure the house. It was done kind of backward. Nobody really thought that it was going to be this wide-open door to criminal activity.

We need to change the equation for cybercriminals. Right now the chances are they won't get caught; cybercrime offers criminals huge benefit at very little cost. Law enforcement needs to recruit young people who can match skills with the criminals. We also need to work closely with foreign governments and agencies to better identify, deter, and apprehend cybercriminals. We need to make examples of them.

Improving our cybercrime prevention means a lot more talent, a lot more resources, a lot more hands-on collaboration with countries on the outskirts—Russia, China, even Israel. These are the countries that are constantly trying to penetrate our cyberspace. And even if we are able to identify the person overseas, we still need the cooperation of the overseas government and law enforcement to help us find and apprehend the person. Electrical grids are extremely vulnerable to cyber attacks. Utilities built long before the Internet need engineering retrofits to make them better able to withstand attacks.

As with cybercrime, efforts against terrorism must be coordinated to be effective. Communication is crucial among all levels of law enforcement, from local law enforcement and national agencies sharing information—in both directions—to a similar international flow of information among different countries' governments and national bureaus.

In the U.S., since 9/11, the FBI and local law enforcement now share a lot more information with each other locally and nationally. Internationally, as well, we are sharing more information with Interpol and other intelligence and law enforcement agencies throughout the world to be able to better detect, identify, and prevent criminal activity.

When it comes to terrorism, we also need to ramp up our public relations. Preventing terror attacks takes more than a military response. We need to address this culture of death with our own Internet media campaign and 800 numbers to make it easy for people to reach out to law enforcement and help build the critical human infrastructure. Without people, there are no leads—people on the inside of a criminal enterprise are essential to directing law enforcement resources effectively, telling you when to listen, where to watch, and which accounts to check.

In New York City, the populace is well aware of the "see something, say something" campaign. Still, we need to do more. More people need to speak up. Again, it comes down to trusting your instincts. If someone seems a little off to you, find a law enforcement representative and share your perception. Listen to your gut. Your gut will always tell you: there's something hinky going on here. Human beings have a sixth sense that goes back to our caveman days when animals used to hunt us. So take action, talk to law enforcement when something about a person makes you uneasy or you feel something around you isn't right.

We have to be prepared not just on the prevention side but in terms of responses. Almost every workplace conducts a fire drill at least once a year. We need to do the same with active-shooter drills. Property managers today may even have their own highly trained active-shooter teams, ready to be on site within minutes of any attack.

We will never stop crime, but we can contain the harm it causes. The coordinated efforts of law enforcement, an alert and well-trained citizenry, and the smart use of DNA, facial profiles, and fingerprinting will go a long way toward reducing the number and severity of terror events.

Be it the prevention of street crime or cybercrime, gang violence or terrorism, sharing information is essential. Only then can we put our technology to good use. People are key to detection and prevention. Without the human element, I like to say a camera's going to take a pretty picture of somebody committing a crime.

Law enforcement must strive to attract qualified people with the right instincts, team-sensibility, and work ethic. At the end of the day, there's no hunting like the hunting of man. It's a thrill; it's a rush; and that to me is law enforcement in its purest form.

MANNY GOMEZ, Esq.

President of MG Security Services,

Chairman of the National Law Enforcement Association,

former FBI Special Agent,

U.S. Marine, and NYPD Sergeant

CHAPTER 1

WHAT INTELLIGENCE AGENCIES DO

Words to Understand

Bug: a concealed listening device

Covert: secret, undercover

Harbor (v.): to give shelter or refuge to

Subversive: a systematic attempt to overthrow or undermine a government or political system by persons working secretly from within

ALMOST EVERY DEVELOPED COUNTRY IN THE WORLD INCLUDES AN INTELLIGENCE AGENCY AS AN ESSENTIAL PART OF ITS GOVERNMENT APPARATUS. IN MOST COUNTRIES, THE POLICE PROVIDE THE MAIN SOURCE OF DOMESTIC LAW-AND-ORDER ENFORCEMENT. DIPLOMATIC RELATIONS ABROAD PROVIDE THE MAIN FORUM FOR RELATIONSHIPS BETWEEN COUNTRIES. INTELLIGENCE AGENCIES, HOWEVER, WORK BY SECRET OR UNDERCOVER OPERATION, ENABLING THEM TO GATHER INFORMATION THAT MIGHT OTHERWISE BE HIDDEN OR SUPPRESSED. IN THIS WAY, INTELLIGENCE AGENCIES ARE VITAL FOR GOVERNMENT POLICY MAKING,

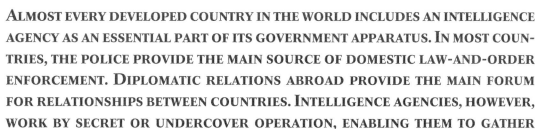

The seal in the lobby of the George Bush Center for Intelligence in Langley, Virginia. The official CIA headquarters is named for former President George H. W. Bush, Director of the CIA from 1976 to 1977.

9

PROVIDING GOVERNMENTS, THE POLICE, AND THE MILITARY WITH ESSENTIAL DETAILS, ANALYSIS, AND INFORMATION ON THE ACTIVITIES OF SUBVERSIVE DOMESTIC GROUPS OR THE HIDDEN AGENDAS OF FOREIGN COUNTRIES.

Intelligence agencies play a unique and highly specialized role in safeguarding national security, preventing the spread of illegal arms and nuclear weaponry, and in combating global drug trafficking.

Knowledge of the Enemy

Intelligence work can be broadly defined as "knowledge of the enemy," and many of its techniques and priorities were formed under conditions of war. Most intelligence agencies today can date their origins to the mass intelligence activities of World War II. However, intelligence work is also essential for nations that are at peace, providing clues to overseas economic policies, and working in unison with other countries' intelligence agencies to ensure that international terrorists or drug or arms dealers are not being inadvertently **harbored**. Intelligence agencies are expert in monitoring such activities as money laundering, smuggling, and fraud. Gathering information from an international intelligence network and shared community of databases and information, intelligence agencies working together are the most effective way to anticipate and prevent terrorist strikes and global crime.

Intelligence agencies support the work of government and collect information for government use from what is known as "the field," or territories, either throughout the domestic territory or overseas. Such information might be formed under the cover of overseas diplomacy, where diplomatic relations may yield special insight. Intelligence is also gathered from the interception of communications, by means of planted **bugs**, or listening devices, or via "listening stations," which pick up fax or e-mail messages by means of cable transmission or satellite detection. Satellite and aerial photography is also of extreme significance in intelligence work, enabling agents to assess the buildup of military activity throughout the world and to monitor nuclear testing in the arms race. However, intelligence agencies do not simply gather information.

The Abwehr Enigma cipher machine. Obtaine by the Allies, it helped codebreakers to break seemingly impossibly complex German code at Bletchley Park, Milton Keynes, in England during World War II.

Aerial photograph showing a missile assembly facility in Cuba in 1962, taken by the CIA just before the Cuban Missile Crisis. Today, intelligence agencies mainly use satellite technology to produce imagery of virtually infinite levels of detail.

They are highly trained in interpreting information and putting it into context to work out its significance. By constantly collecting and interpreting information in the public domain—for example, newspaper and television news—intelligence agents can tie public information to more secret state or government information. Intelligence agencies look for the inside story and will work undercover to obtain it. In many ways, their work resembles the work of news gatherers, with the exception that they do not seek to sensationalize or sell their information. Intelligence agencies are agents of their government and are strictly monitored and controlled by government committees.

Attack cannot always be prevented, but specialist antiterrorist intelligence forces are essential to any country menaced by terrorist strikes. Shown here is the aftermath of an Irish Republican Army (IRA) bomb blast at the Docklands Light Railway, London in February 1996.

Nevertheless, in pursuing the interests of their governments, they may break the laws of other governments to get information. Consequently, intelligence work has also been defined as "the organized theft of information."

Combating Terrorist Activity

Intelligence agents do not generally spy on their own people, although they may monitor subversive or potentially dangerous domestic organizations, such as antigovernment groups. However, the degree to which an intelligence agency uses devious and sometimes forceful means depends very much on the state of the country and the level of the threat. For example, where territory is disputed, an intelligence agency may become more belligerent, or warlike. In Israel, where Palestinian territories are occupied, the intelligence agency Mossad applies military intelligence to combat terrorist organizations, such as the Palestinian Liberation Organization, Hamas, Fatah, and The Popular Front for the Liberation of Palestine. The same has been true of British intelligence agencies working to counter the terrorist activities of the Irish Republican Army.

Responsibilities

Government intelligence agencies or services are generally responsible for the following areas:

- Gathering information to avert dangers to state security
- General counterespionage
- Averting possible threats to the armed forces
- Gathering information about situations abroad
- Analyzing secret intelligence regarding threats
- Enabling others—for example, the police and the military—to act to counter threats to national security.
- Advising the government and keeping the military and police informed of threats and of appropriate security measures
- Assisting in all other government investigative work by providing relevant information

Because intelligence work is vital to national security, the classic targets of espionage are military secrets, environmental government secrets, and information regarding threats to other governments. This information might consist of new weapons systems, military strategies, or information about the stationing of troops. Information on foreign or monetary policies or any information revealing internal tensions in a government is also valued by decision-makers. In combating crime, intelligence agents work undercover to check the flow of illegal drugs into and out of the country or to interrupt terrorist activities before they occur.

Safeguarding Global and National Security

Secrecy and deception are major factors in intelligence work. Most intelligence operations must be secret, or **covert**, because only by stealth can information that an enemy wants to hide be discovered. Intelligence work relies on building a detailed and long-term picture of enemy activities and requires many years of information-gathering and analysis. Countries will often actively attempt to blur the picture that another government has of its economic or military activities. For this reason, intelligence agencies are continually adjusting their assessments. In other words, the picture is never static, but is constantly evolving. Intelligence agencies must keep pace with every new development and change over time.

Here, a member of the Irish Republican Army (IRA) practices with a homemade rocket launcher. Such groups are difficult for the intelligence agencies to infiltrate because of their roots in the local community.

Kenyans study a United States "wanted" notice for a mastermind of Rwanda's genocide. Intelligence agencies often work in global unison to combat terror and to safeguard each others' national security.

Providing information for policy-makers, intelligence agencies do not themselves make policy decisions. Their advice is, however, generally noted when foreign-policy decisions are made. Intelligence agencies are also important sources of technological advances, developing new methods of capturing and analyzing information, and contributing to sophisticated levels of law enforcement training. For all these reasons, intelligence agencies are a vital part of government activity and a necessary component for national, and sometimes global, security.

Text-Dependent Questions

1. What is intelligence?
2. What do intelligence agencies do?
3. What is espionage?

Research Projects

1. Why is it important to have intelligence agencies?
2. Why must espionage be covert? How do intelligence agencies maintain secrecy?
3. Who was Mata Hari? Learn about her life and her career as a spy.

INTELLIGENCE AGENTS

Words to Understand

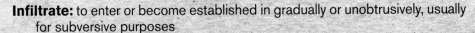

Infiltrate: to enter or become established in gradually or unobtrusively, usually for subversive purposes

Linguistic: relating to language

Paramilitary: of, relating to, being, or characteristic of a force formed on a military pattern, especially as a potential auxiliary military force

INTELLIGENCE AGENTS ARE USUALLY CITIZENS OF THE STATE FOR WHICH THEY WORK. SOMETIMES, FOREIGN AGENTS ARE USED FOR REASONS OF CULTURAL ASSIMILATION OR LANGUAGE. FOR EXAMPLE, THE ISRAELI INTELLIGENCE AGENCY MOSSAD FREQUENTLY DEPLOYS JEWS BORN IN ARAB COUNTRIES TO BLEND INTO ARAB SOCIETY AND GATHER SECRET OR PERTINENT INFORMATION. MOST INTELLIGENCE AGENTS WORKING OVERSEAS OPERATE UNDER THE COVER OF DIPLOMACIES AND GAIN A STRONG WORKING KNOWLEDGE OF THE OVERSEAS COUNTRY AND ITS PEOPLE.

Intelligence agents often have either military or police backgrounds, or are highly educated university graduates with scientific, engineering, analytical, or **linguistic** training. Not all agents work in the "field," and different skills are required for different kinds of intelligence work. The vast amount of intelligence

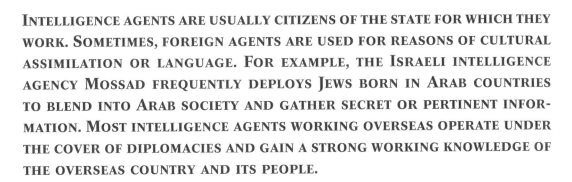

At the Al Najah University in the West Bank, Palestinian students stand in front of giant pro-Palestinian liberation Hamas posters. All potentially subversive groups and individuals are closely monitored by Israeli intelligence.

17

ata processing and office work, and involves collecting and entering into rmation in the public domain, such as news or television reports. Intelligence ork on analysis and who interpret raw data are among the most intellectually in the world, using logic, analysis, and deductive and inductive techniques to hypothesize accurately.

Recruiting Intelligence Agents

Information scientists are of enormous importance in intelligence work, where the accurate interpretation of data is crucial. Skills such as seeking, acquiring, and organizing information, as well as information scientists' ability to recognize patterns in what might otherwise appear to be random pieces of data, are the important skills that librarians and information scientists bring to intelligence work.

In British intelligence, code-breaking ability is of great importance. Britain manages the world's most significant listening stations at GCHQ (Government Communications Headquarters), Cheltenham and Menwith Hill. GCHQ has a history of employing the most analytical, lateral minds, working on some of the most challenging intelligence tasks in the world, and recruits technologists, mathematicians, intelligence analysts, librarians and information scientists, and linguists.

In the United States, intelligence agency officers must usually have a graduate degree and must be an American citizen. Anyone applying for an intelligence job will be thoroughly investigated by means of an extensive background check. This includes an investigation of the applicant's life history, taking into account political or ideological allegiances, character, and soundness of judgment. A medical examination is also required. The CIA (Central Intelligence Agency) and FBI (Federal Bureau of Investigation) have extremely stringent drug policies, and usually reject anyone who has used drugs in recent years. Such thorough background checks mean that applications to intelligence agencies can take more than a year to process.

In the United States, the CIA is particularly interested in candidates with backgrounds in Central Eurasian, East Asian, and Middle Eastern languages and cultures or degrees in international business/finance/relations, economics, physical science, or nuclear/ biological/ chemical engineering. Having a university degree is not mandatory, but is highly recommended. Overseas officers, intelligence analysts, and other nonclerical positions must have a college degree, preferably an advanced degree, such as a PhD.

Recruiting and Training New Candidates

Other qualities that the CIA lists as essential are "impeccable personal integrity, strong interpersonal skills, the ability to handle ambiguity, the ability to take calculated risks," and foreign language proficiency. The CIA states that "integrity, character, and patriotism are a must."

Specially trained operators monitor supercomputers at CIA headquarters.CIA personnel are highly skilled at operating software and in analytical reasoning.

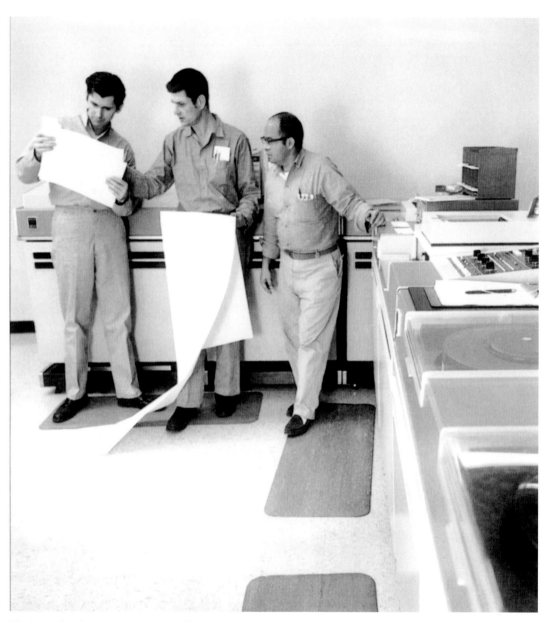

The logical and accurate analysis of data has always been a necessary requirement for intelligence work. Here, surrounded by the more cumbersome technology of the day, FBI agents of the 1970s are examining a data report.

An aerial view of the CIA headquarters in Langley, Virginia. Although CIA agents operate throughout the world, this is where computer network management, databases, and general communications are centrally coordinated.

Applicants accepted into the CIA professional trainee (PT) program are assigned to Washington, D.C. for 18 months, during which time they will spend nine months at two disciplines–Operations Desk Officer and Collection Management Officer. At the end of the program, trainees are assessed and evaluated for movement into the clandestine service trainee (CST) program, the program that prepares trainees for overseas work as either an Operations Officer or Collection Management Officer.

In the United States, the FBI recruits scientists, computer specialists, and other specialized personnel at its forensic laboratory, engineering research facility, and the criminal justice information services division. The FBI runs a strict drug policy. Every applicant who successfully completes the initial application process is required to complete a polygraph examination (also know as a lie detector) in order to continue processing, as well as drug testing. A comprehensive background investigation then takes place. This includes credit and criminal checks, interviews of colleagues and friends, contacts with personal and business references, interviews of past and current employers and neighbors, and verification of birth, citizenship, and educational achievements. Routine background checks are carried out on all FBI agents as a matter of course.

Gathering Intelligence Using Paramilitary Procedures

In times of heightened military or defense activity, or at times in which security may be strained by the threat of international terrorism, certain branches of intelligence work may take on a **paramilitary** aspect. In such cases, intelligence agents may be forced to use blackmail and manipulation tactics. The Israeli intelligence agency Mossad has forced Palestinians in the occupied territories into informing on their neighbors, while British intelligence agencies have put similar pressure on individuals from both the Catholic and Protestant communities in Northern Ireland.

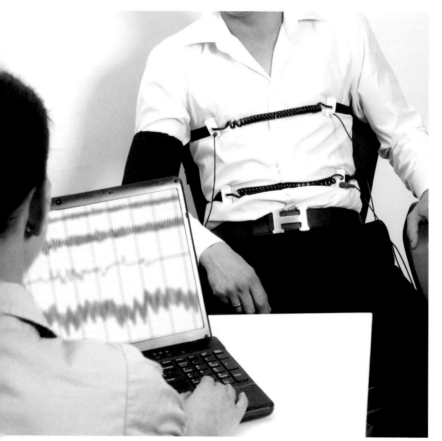

Recruitment to the Federal Bureau of Investigation requires lengthy background checks and interviews. Lie detector examinations are only the start of the process.

Joining the FBI

The FBI will exclude any applicant on the following grounds:

- Lack of U.S. citizenship
- Conviction of a felony
- Default on student loans
- Failure to register for the Selective Service System (males)
- Failure of a drug test
- Violation of the FBI Employment Drug Policy, which disqualifies anyone who has used marijuana in the past three years, any other illegal drug within the past ten years, sold or distributed any illegal drug, or abused prescription drugs within the past three years.

The United States is probably more scrupulous with background checks regarding previous human-rights abuses, or what is known as an "unsavory background." The issue of human-rights abuse is currently highly controversial in the intelligence community. In war zones, agents must be prepared to **infiltrate** enemy communities. They may not only be forced to take arms, but also to extract information from potential informants. Working undercover, they may betray the trust of the community that they infiltrate at any time.

Following the terrorist attacks on the Pentagon and the World Trade Center of September 11, 2001, a new U.S. Intelligence Authorization Act was passed on October 5, 2001. This authorized vital extra funding to intelligence organizations, including the Central Intelligence Agency, the National Security Agency, and the Federal Bureau of Investigation. This funding has been used to push an intensive drive for more aggressive recruiting of international intelligence agents.

An Israeli soldier checks the ID cards of ordinary Palestinians in Hebron. In conflict and occupied zones, the military relies heavily on its intelligence gathering and on ID checks in order to anticipate the movements of potentially subversive individuals.

Workers clear up the debris of the Twin Towers at Ground Zero in New York City after the terrible devastation caused by the terrorist attacks of September 11, 2001.

Text-Dependent Questions

1. What backgrounds are common among intelligence agents?
2. What skills are important to U.S. intelligence agencies?
3. What can disqualify a candidate from the FBI?

Research Projects

1. Why do intelligence agencies do such thorough background checks on would-be agents?
2. Look at the recruiting pages for the CIA and the FBI. If you wanted a career with one of those agencies, how should you start preparing yourself?
3. Investigate code breaking. How do codes work? How do modern intelligence agencies go about breaking them?

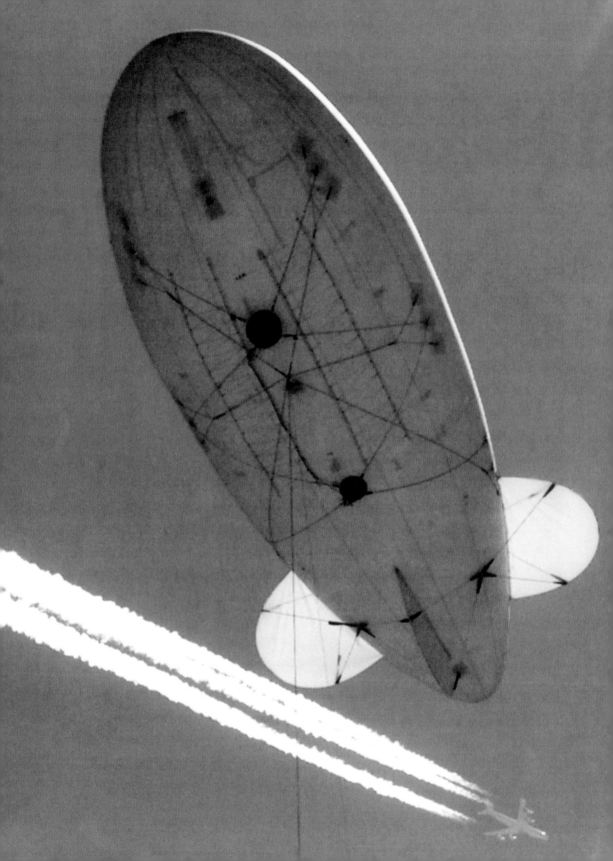

CHAPTER 3

INTELLIGENCE TECHNOLOGY

Words to Understand

Cold War: the lengthy confrontation between Soviet-led Communist Eastern Europe (and China) and the democratic countries of the West, which dominated world politics through much of the second half of the 20th century

Fixations: fixed installations or concentrations of military activity

Logistic: the handling of the details of an operation, including the maintenance, transportation, and storage of goods and materials

Morse lamp: a lamp used for communicating the Morse code through a series of flashes at different speeds and at varying intervals to express different letters of the alphabet

INTELLIGENCE AGENCIES MAY DEPEND ON MANPOWER OR HUMAN RESOURCES IN ORDER TO GATHER INFORMATION IN THE FIELD, BUT THEY ALSO RELY ON TECHNOLOGY FOR GATHERING INFORMATION. IN FACT, TECHNOLOGICAL SURVEILLANCE IS GENERALLY CONSIDERED THE MOST EFFICIENT AND ECONOMIC WAY OF COLLECTING VITAL CLUES AS TO GEOGRAPHIC MILITARY BUILDUPS OR ACTIVITY. THIS KIND OF TECHNOLOGY IS CALLED SURVEILLANCE TECHNOLOGY. AGENTS MAKE USE OF SUCH TECHNOLOGY IN THEIR WORK,

An Israeli airplane passes a surveillance blimp equipped with a video camera. Aerial cameras provide vital real-time data for intelligence and military interpretation during conflicts.

BOTH IN THE FIELD AND IN ANALYSIS. INTELLIGENCE AGENTS INTERCEPT COMMUNICATIONS, TAP PHONES, STORE IMPORTANT INFORMATION IN VAST DATABASES, USE TECHNOLOGY IN FORENSIC WORK, AND RELY ON SATELLITE LINKS FOR AERIAL PHOTOGRAPHY AND NEWS TRANSMISSION. INTELLIGENCE AGENCIES ARE ALSO AT THE CUTTING EDGE OF TECHNOLOGICAL INNOVATION AND USE SOME OF THE MOST SOPHISTICATED PROTECTIVE AND SECURITY MEASURES EVER DEVISED.

All surveillance technology relies on intercepting communication. Communication can take place through several different mediums:
- Air (sound waves)
- Light (**morse lamp**, fiber-optic cable)
- Electric current (telegraph, telephone)
- Electromagnetic waves (all forms of radio, cell phones)
- Computer networks and Internet
- Video (security cameras, drones, satellites)

Any third party that succeeds in accessing the medium can intercept the communications and read or interpret the content.

Surveillance technology developed largely as a response to war. It breaks down into three main areas:
- SIGINT–Signals Intelligence
- IMINT–Imagery Intelligence
- MASINT–Measurement and Signature Intelligence

SIGINT—Signals Intelligence

Signals Intelligence was developed during the Second World War, when enemy radio waves were intercepted for the first time. Today, satellite interception systems are used mainly for interception purposes. Signals detected can reveal the location of air defenses and missile forces, and signals can also be used to relay messages between foreign agents working in unison across the world. Filters are used to isolate the signal to be analyzed. For this reason, voice registration technology is of growing importance in the field of government surveillance.

Britain is the global leader in Signals Intelligence, but the United States, as a close ally, is one of the main users of Britain's special "listening stations," GCHQ and Menwith Hill.

A testimony about bugging devices during the Senate Watergate hearings of 1973. The use of bugging devices has remained controversial since the **Cold War.**

IMINT—Imagery Intelligence

Aerial photography dates from the use of hot air balloons for observation during the American Civil War and from German experiments using kites and rockets as platforms in the late 1800s. It has become increasingly important as technology improves, and imagery gathered by stealth-plane photography was used to identify strategic targets for the U.S. Air Force in both the Korean and Vietnam wars during the 1950s and 1960s. During operations Desert Shield and Desert Storm in the Gulf War of the 1990s, the information provided by imagery, including that broadcast by satellite link, played an important role at both the tactical and strategic levels.

Today, Imagery Intelligence, or IMINT, involves images gathered by satellite, but also by surveillance cameras placed in a wide variety of locations, including aircraft and drones. These pictures may be broad and panoramic, revealing defense buildups or military training grounds as seen from the air.

Algebraic-formulas imagery can be used to measure objects on the ground—for example, in estimating the storage capacity of **logistic** military sites. Imagery used can also be incredibly detailed, showing a particular license plate on a car, or even a picture of a human face.

Vast databases access national and departmental collection-management data, providing full geographic area coverage. Imagery-intelligence work primarily consists of researching data and creating new surveillance targets from which to gather information. The position of the satellite is altered accordingly as new targets for surveillance are identified. Image enhancement, image manipulation, simultaneous manipulation, stereo capabilities, image comparison, and image warping are other important technological areas in imagery intelligence.

Today, imagery can be easily stored, retrieved, enhanced, and distributed. High-quality still images from live video can be created, enhanced, and edited for detailed analysis. Aerial or satellite images with latitude and longitude references even make it possible to achieve high-magnification and zooming, and global databases then enable such information to be easily shared.

Intercepting Communications

- Conversations can be picked up by a microphone (a bug) hidden in a room. Laser equipment that picks up vibrations on window-panes can also be used.

- Screens that emit radiation can be picked up from a distance of 100 feet (30 m).

- Telephones, fax machines, and e-mail messages can be tapped by use of cables.

- Communications from a cell phone can be intercepted.

- Closed-circuit communications can also be intercepted within certain radio ranges.

MASINT–Measurement and Signature Intelligence

Measurement and Signature Intelligence (MASINT) is scientific and technical intelligence information achieved by mathematical analysis of data gathered from specific technical sensors. The collection, analysis, and management of signature data on military vehicles, ships, and aircraft is vital to the development and evaluation of advanced sensor and weapons systems, which must not only detect and track potential targets, but also distinguish between friendly and hostile systems.

MASINT includes:
- Radar Intelligence (RADINT)
- Acoustic Intelligence (ACOUSTINT)
- Nuclear Intelligence (NUCINT)
- Radio Frequency/Electromagnetic Pulse Intelligence (RF/EMPINT)
- Electro-Optical Intelligence (ELECTRO-OPTINT)
- Laser Intelligence (LASINT)
- Materials Intelligence
- Unintentional Radiation Intelligence (RINT)
- Chemical and Biological Intelligence (CBINT)
- Directed Energy Weapons Intelligence (DEWINT)
- Effluent/Debris Collection
- Spectroscopic Intelligence
- Infrared Intelligence (IRINT)

The Lockheed TR-1 is a later development of the famous U2 spy plane. Designed for tactical reconnaissance in Europe, the TR-1 is one of the main intelligence-gathering aircraft of U.S. military and intelligence services.

Such measurements can provide vital clues as to the source of a signal and can be analyzed to provide information on the whereabouts of an enemy force or on its weapons capability.

Encryption

Intercepted conversations provide the bulk of the raw data, but decoding-encryption software forms a major and highly complex aspect of intelligence work. Encryption scrambles electronic communications and information, and in this way functions as a code, protecting secret or vulnerable information from exploitation. For this reason, learning to break software and encryption codes is important for intelligence agencies to master, and significant government resources are deployed to this end in special intelligence-agency training programs. Encryption research and development is an important investment, especially given the phenomenon of computer hacking and industrial espionage.

Significant Satellite Systems Worldwide

As of 2015, there were over 1200 operational satellites orbiting Earth (along with about 2600 satellites that no longer work but are still in orbit). Many of these are operated by government agencies for weather forecasting or as part of the Global Positioning System (GPS). A number are used for communications. Many others are privately owned and used for surveillance; the companies that own them sell the images to law enforcement and intelligence agencies. From space, satellites can pick up public cable networks from one part of the world and feed them into cable networks in another, meaning that most broadcasts can be intercepted from anywhere in the world. The main satellite systems used by government intelligence agencies are:

- INTELSAT (International Telecommunications Satellite Organization), used by 144 governments and operating a fleet of 19 geostationary satellites that cover the Atlantic, Indian, and Pacific regions.
- INTERSPUTNIK, a former agency of the former Soviet Union, with 24 member countries and some 40 users, including France and Britain. Its satellites are owned by the Russian Federation and cover the Atlantic, Indian, and Pacific regions.
- INMARSAT (Interim International Maritime Satellite), which provides mobile worldwide communications at sea. Its headquarters are in London, and it has nine satellites that cover the entire globe.
- EUTELSAT, the European regional communication satellite system, which is based in Paris. It has 40 member countries and 18 satellites that cover Europe,

Africa, and large parts of Asia, and also forms links with America. It is mainly used for private networks and press agencies, such as Reuters.

Satellite Intelsat 905 preparing to launch at the European Space Agency Launch Center in Kourou, French Guiana. An international system, Intelsat circles the earth, gathering information that will be made available to many different governments.

There are several alternatives to EUTELSAT. ARABSAT is the Arab regional counterpart to EUTELSAT, made up of 21 Arab countries. PALAPA is the Indonesian system, in operation since 1995, and is the South Asian counterpart to EUTELSAT, covering Malaysia, China, Japan, India, Pakistan, and other countries in the region. National satellite systems include the French TELECOM; ITALSAT, with reception possible only in Italy; AMOS, the Israeli satellite covering the Middle East; and HISPASAT, covering Spain and Portugal.

Operating "Colossus" at Bletchley Park during World War II. The machine was a forerunner to the modern-day computer and made invaluable contributions to the Allied victory.

A U.S. Air Force B2 Spirit stealth bomber used in the Operation Allied Air Force, undertaken in the former Yugoslavia in 1999. In conflict, military forces rely heavily on intelligence when trying to identify targets suitable for attack.

Mystery Aircraft

Mystery aircraft are secret aircraft that can dodge interception devices and fly over enemy terrain, taking photographs. Today, many are flown by remote control without a pilot. The history of mystery aircraft dates back to the Cold War. Early models included the U2, the SR-71 Senior Crown/Blackbird, F-l 17A Senior Trend/Nighthawk, and the B2 Advanced Technology Bomber/Stealth Bomber.

Important technological advances were made during the Gulf War. Here, a U.S. Air Force Nighthawk aircraft, equipped with weapons, is used for the first time in the Persian Gulf as part of a stealth operation.

The United States used these aircraft to fly over the Soviet Union, China, and Vietnam. Their development, production, and flights were shrouded in secrecy and were barely publicized. In May 1960, however, a U2 piloted by Francis Gary Powers was shot down. This drew attention to the use of these planes by the United States. In 1984, the crash of one of the aircraft that year and another crash in 1986 drew further attention to the planes' existence and roused global controversy. As the Cold War ended, these planes were taken out of service, but after the Iraqi invasion of Kuwait in August 1990, the use of such planes has been rising.

An Unmanned Aerial Vehicle (UAV), better known as a drone, is a remotely piloted or self-piloted aircraft that can carry cameras, sensors, or communications equipment. Aircraft without a pilot, whether as aerial targets or used in military operations, date back to World War I. They have been used in a reconnaissance and intelligence-gathering role since the 1950s, and are increasingly used in combat missions. Since 1964, the U.S. Defense Department and the U.S. Navy have been actively developing new systems. Interest in the UAV waned through the 1970s and 1980s, but reemerged during operations Desert Shield and Desert Storm in the Gulf War. Today, at least 14 countries are using or developing over 76 different types of surveillance, target acquisition, electronic warfare, and expendable UAVs. In the 2010s drone technology took off, and the devices were widely used for remote attacks and surveillance.

Technology enables intelligence agencies to bring together details to make a global picture of any significant **fixations** and movements. The United States and the United Kingdom participate in an agreement called USUSA that sets up international signals intelligence project. Participating nations include Canada, Australia, and New Zealand, though other nations share the data as well. The organization is sometimes called Five Eyes. Though the work of this network is kept largely secret, in 2013 Edward Snowden revealed that the National

A Predator Unmanned Aerial Vehicle, a UAV or drone, takes off from the coast of Southern California on a U.S. Naval reconnaissance mission. The Predator provides infrared and color video imagery to intelligence analysts and controllers working from the ground and at sea.

Security Agency (NSA) was monitoring a vast array of communications, some at very high levels.

Text-Dependent Questions

1. What is surveillance?
2. What are some methods of aerial surveillance?
3. What is a satellite?

Research Projects

1. Surveillance involves collecting information on people who do not know they are being watched. Where should an agency draw the line between collecting information and respecting the privacy of the people they are watching?
2. Which satellites provide surveillance images? How high are they, and who operates them? How detailed are the images they provide? What areas can they cover?
3. Investigate encryption. How does this protect secure data? How can an intelligence agency get around it?

CHAPTER 4

UNITED STATES INTELLIGENCE AGENCIES

Words to Understand

Collude: to conspire or plot

Cryptology: the science and art of making and breaking codes and ciphers

Dissident: someone who disagrees with an established religious or political system, organization, or belief

Jurisdiction: the power, right, or authority to interpret and apply the law

Telemetry: the science or process of transmitting data

White-collar crime: crime committed by office staff, usually involving theft from the company they work for

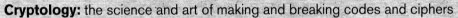

THE MOST FAMOUS U.S. INTELLIGENCE AGENCIES ARE THE CENTRAL INTELLIGENCE AGENCY, OR THE CIA, AND THE FEDERAL BUREAU OF INVESTIGATION, OR THE FBI. HOWEVER, ALL AGENCIES COMBINE TO SUPPORT THE U.S. GOVERNMENT BY KEEPING IT FULLY INFORMED OF USEFUL INTELLIGENCE INFORMATION THAT HAS BEEN GATHERED BOTH AT HOME AND ABROAD.

An intelligence specialist in World War II, Allen Dulles later served as deputy director and then as director of the newly founded U.S. Central Intelligence Agency. He promoted the use of the U2 spy plane after 1955 in order to monitor Soviet activity at a time of Cold War tensions.

The 13 main intelligence agencies are:
- Air Force Intelligence
- Army Intelligence
- The Central Intelligence Agency
- The National Imagery and Mapping Agency
- Defense Intelligence Agency
- The Department of Energy's Office of Intelligence and Counterintelligence
- Department of State: Bureau of Intelligence and Research
- The Federal Bureau of Investigation
- Marine Corps Intelligence
- Naval Intelligence
- National Reconnaissance Office
- National Security Agency
- The Treasury Department Office of Intelligence and Analysis

The CIA seal, designed in 1949, features the symbolic emblems of the shield and the American eagle.

Air Force Intelligence

Air Force Intelligence operates the National Air Intelligence Center (NAIC) and produces intelligence on aerospace systems and data on the capabilities and intentions of potential enemies. Air-intelligence agents accompany each U.S. Air Force team, using high-tech sensor systems and airborne reconnaissance systems, such as the U2 and RC-135, to gather vital information.

Army Intelligence

Army Intelligence provides commanders with the capability to communicate with and receive intelligence from many intelligence agencies around the world in order to ensure mission success.

Defense Intelligence Agency

The Defense Intelligence Agency (DIA) is the senior military-intelligence component of the intelligence community. Established in 1961, the primary mission of the DIA is to provide all-source intelligence to the U.S. armed forces. The objectives of the DIA are:
- Battle-damage assessment.
- Targeting weapons proliferation.
- Warning of impending crises.

- Maintenance of databases on foreign military organizations and their equipment.
- Providing support to peacekeeping operations.
- Providing support to UN (United Nations) operations and U.S. allies.
- Advising policy makers in the Department of Defense and members of the Joint Chiefs of Staff.
- Providing information on foreign weapons systems to American weapons planners and the weapons-acquisition community.

The DIA coordinates and combines military-intelligence analysis for defense officials and military commanders worldwide. The DIA has been directly involved in crises in places like Somalia, Haiti, Bosnia, Rwanda, Iraq, and North Korea, as well as such global challenges as the proliferation of weapons of mass destruction, terrorism, drug trafficking, and the monitoring of arms-control treaties.

Here, a member of the Tactical Psychological Operations Team, a unit promoting cooperation from civilians, interviews Afghan civilians. Although interpreters are sometimes used in the field, fluency in the spoken language in intelligence work is highly desirable.

Department of Energy

The Department of Energy's involvement in the intelligence community dates from the post-World War II atomic age. It has numerous goals in national security, and part of its mission is to contribute to the policy and institutional leadership necessary to achieve a secure national defense.

Department of State: Bureau of Intelligence and Research

The Bureau of Intelligence and Research (INR) comprises a group of global analysts working on behalf of the State Department and was originally established in 1946. INR's order is to inform policy-makers, and it provides the focal point within the State Department for all policy issues and activities involving the intelligence community. INR derives its information base from diplomatic reporting and U.S. and foreign scholars, and aims to provide early warning and in-depth analysis of events and trends that affect U.S. foreign policy and national security interests.

Mission of the Department of Energy

These are the stated missions of the Department of Energy:

- To provide the Department and other U.S. government policy-makers and decision-makers with timely, accurate, high-impact, foreign-intelligence analyses.
- To detect and defeat foreign intelligence services bent on acquiring sensitive information on the Department's programs, facilities, technology, and personnel.
- To provide technical and analytical support to the Director of Central Intelligence (DCI).
- To make the Department's technical and analytical expertise available to other members of the intelligence community.

The Department's intelligence responsibility includes areas such as nuclear proliferation, nuclear weapons technology, fossil and nuclear energy, and science and technology.

INR focuses on unstable regimes, emerging former Soviet-bloc economies, trade competitors, and military proliferation and terrorism in major conflict zones as well as around the world. INR sits on the National Counterintelligence Policy Board and works with the Bureau of Diplomatic Security on security matters. Significantly, INR develops intelligence policy for the Department of State and maintains policy continuity between intelligence activities overseas and domestic U.S. policy.

Marine Corps Intelligence

The Marine Corps Intelligence Activity (MCIA) works together with Naval Intelligence and Coast Guard Intelligence in the National Maritime Intelligence Center and at the Marine Corps base in Quantico, Virginia. These locations make the best use of the U.S. infrastructure.

Marines in full combat equipment. The success of their mission will depend on communications from the Marines Corps Intelligence Activity, Naval Intelligence, and Coast Guard Intelligence.

Radar-approach-control air traffic controllers at the U.S. Incirlik Air Base in Turkey. Radar watch requires sophisticated technology and can provide vital intelligence data.

Naval Intelligence

The Office of Naval Intelligence (ONI), located primarily in the National Maritime Intelligence Center in Suitland, Maryland, is the centralized base for global maritime intelligence. ONI provides expertise ranging from the analysis of acoustic information on foreign sensor systems, to ocean surveillance systems, submarine platforms, and undersea weapons systems. It appraises opposition to maritime combat tactics and provides an authoritative resource for maritime air issues. It is also the leading informant on global merchant affairs and a national leader in other nontraditional maritime issues, such as counternarcotics, fishing rights issues, ocean dumping of radioactive waste, technology transfer, and counterproliferation. ONI is also engaged in developing new weapons systems and countermeasures. Overall, ONI is an invaluable resource to the intelligence community and is the leading authority on maritime capabilities worldwide.

National Reconnaissance Office

The National Reconnaissance Office (NRO) is an agency of the Department of Defense, and its mission is to ensure that the United States has the technological and spaceborne assets needed to acquire intelligence worldwide. NRO's main activities are research, development, acquisition, and operation of the nations intelligence satellites. The NRO helps to monitor arms-control agreements and global military operations and exercises. The Secretary of Defense has the responsibility for the management and operation of the NRO, which is shared with the Director of Central Intelligence. The NRO is staffed by personnel from CIA, the military services, and civilian personnel from the Department of Defense.

National Security Agency

The National Security Agency (NSA) works within the Department of Defense to plan, coordinate, and direct Signals Intelligence. In other words, the National Security Agency decodes secret foreign communications while protecting U.S. secret codes—a capability in which the United States leads the world. Known as **cryptology**, this constitutes the fundamental mission of NSA. NSA's main tasks are to exploit foreign electromagnetic signals and to protect any electronic information critical to U.S. national security. In this way, NSA contributes to the intelligence-information data used by decision-makers and military commanders. Communications consists of:
- Cell phone, telephone or teleprinter message communications
- Electronic communications such as email and social media
- Noncommunications signals, such as radar
- Signals associated with missiles, weapons systems, and space vehicles, known as **telemetry** The NSA protects all classified information stored or sent through U.S. government equipment, including computers, phones, and other devices for sending messages. NSA is also responsible for a large part of intelligence training in the intelligence community and is a leader in training employees of other agencies. The NSA and its Information Assurance Directorate have established a National Cyber Assistance Program to help commercial organizations handle cyber security.

The Treasury Department Office of Intelligence and Analysis

The Office of Intelligence and Analysis is charged with the task of forging strong links between the intelligence community and the officials responsible for international economic policy. The office handles intelligence for the Treasury's decision-makers and customers, looks for threats to networks, and provides security to safeguard Treasury information.

The Federal Bureau of Investigation

The Federal Bureau of Investigation (FBI) is the centrally administered division of the U.S. Department of Justice, and is one of the largest, most powerful and influential law enforcement organizations in the world, containing many offices and divisions under one agency to deal with a wide variety of criminal activities. The FBI is responsible for enforcing federal statutes and for conducting sensitive national security investigations. Special Agents who operate for the FBI are distributed throughout the entire country and are responsible for enforcing federal criminal law. In other words, these agents will investigate a range of crimes, from bank robberies to frauds against the government. The FBI also has responsibility for finding and detaining foreign spies working in the United States and for safeguarding the internal security of the country.

One of the major responsibilities of the FBI is the recovery of fugitives, or those on the run from the law. Searches for FBI fugitives are conducted not just in the United States, but worldwide, and the FBI holds some of the largest databases in the world to this effect.

Julius and Ethel Rosenberg were charged with conspiracy to commit espionage at the height of the Cold War Red Scare. Incarcerated in the New York House of Detention, they were found guilty and were sentenced to death on April 5, 1951.

The Mission of the FBI

The FBI Identification Division holds the world's largest fingerprint file and makes such details available to other law enforcement agencies. The FBI Headquarters (FBIHQ) in Washington, D.C. directs and supports 56 field offices, approximately 400 satellite offices (known as resident agencies), four specialized field installations, and more than 40 foreign liaison posts. In 2015 the FBI ha approximately 35,000 employees, including special agents, intelligence analysts, information technology specialists, language specialists, and scientists.

In the past, the FBI has investigated and arrested subversive immigrants, and it played a prominent role during the Cold War in tracking and arresting Communist sympathizers. Today, top priority has been given to the five areas that affect society the most: counterterrorism, drugs, organized crime, foreign counterintelligence, violent crime, and **white-collar crime**. The FBI is responsible for detecting and counteracting foreign intelligence activities that gather information adversely affecting U.S. national interests of security.

The FBI's mission is to identify and neutralize the threat in the United States posed by terrorists and their supporters, whether domestic in origin or international. The FBI is involved in a wide range of activities, including investigations into organized crime, white-collar crime, public corruption, financial crime, fraud against the government, bribery, copyright matters, violations of civil rights, bank robbery, extortion, kidnapping, air piracy, terrorism, foreign counterintelligence, and interstate criminal activity.

Offices of the FBI

The FBI is organized into a number of main offices. The Office of the General Counsel provides legal advice to the Director and other FBI officials, and coordinates the defense of civil litigation and administrative claims involving the FBI, its personnel, and its records. The Office of Public and Congressional Affairs is responsible for communicating with news media, the general public, scholars, and authors regarding the FBI. As its name suggests, the Administrative Services Division deals with general administration and personnel support, but also manages recruitment programs and selection systems. This office is also responsible for doing the investigations into the background of applicants to the FBI.

The Counterterrorism Division consolidates all FBI counterterrorism initiatives. The National Infrastructure Protection Center (NIPC) and the National Domestic Preparedness Office (NDPO) are assigned to this division. The NIPC provides threat assessments, warnings, investigations, and responses for threats or attacks against the United States. The NDPO is the clearinghouse for state, local, and federal weapons of mass destruction (WMD) information and assistance. It coordinates all federal planning, training, and resources for providing an emergency response in the event of an attack on the United States.

The Criminal Investigative Division covers many areas of criminal activity. It coordinates investigations into organized crime, including drug matters, racketeering, and money laundering. It also deals with violent crimes and tracks down wanted fugitives, including escaped federal prisoners (in some instances), and those fleeing to avoid prosecution. Gang violence, serial murders, kidnappings, and bank robberies also come under its **jurisdiction.**

The Criminal Investigative Division has the power to move across state boundary lines and is responsible for investigating property crimes of an interstate nature, crime on Native American reservations, crimes against U.S. citizens overseas, and the theft of government property. Investigations into white-collar crime, fraud against the government, corruption of public officials, health care fraud, election law violations, business and economic frauds, and corruption crimes, as well as investigations into civil rights violations round off the areas of responsibility of this group.

Because it covers so many different types of crimes, the FBI has a number of specialized offices, including an Art Theft Program, an Asset Forfeiture Program, a Civil Rights Section, a Crimes Against Children Program, a Financial Crimes Section, an Internet Fraud Complaint Center, and a Jewelry and Gem Program.

An FBI agent performs a forensic search after the Branch Davidian disaster in Waco, Texas, 1993. The FBI investigates all major national crimes and incidents.

Further Training and Preparing for the Future

The Criminal Justice Information Services Division is based in Clarksburg, West Virginia, and is the centralized office for state-of-the-art criminal justice information services in the FBI. It manages the Fingerprint Identification Program, the National Crime Information Center Program, and the Uniform Crime Reporting Program. In addition, it houses the Integrated Automated Fingerprint Identification System (IAFIS), a highly advanced computer-based fingerprint database system. The Next Generation Identification system and Biometric Technology Center use even more advanced methods of identification.

The FBI also keeps an eye on its own staff and has a specific office

FBI recruits are required to undergo New Agent Training at the FBI Academy Quantico, Virginia. Agents are shown here practicing arresting and handcuffin

for this job. The Inspection Division is responsible for reviewing FBI activities to ensure that the conduct of FBI personnel complies with the law.

Preparing for the unexpected and being flexible in response to unusual threats is another important job for the FBI. The Investigative Services Division includes an Information, Analysis, and Assessments section that works to identify and combat future security threats.

The Laboratory Division houses one of the largest and most comprehensive crime laboratories in the world and holds the only full-service federal forensic laboratory. Laboratory activities include crime-scene searches, special surveillance photography, latent-fingerprint examinations, forensic examinations of evidence (including DNA testing), court testimony, and other scientific and technical services.

The National Security Division coordinates investigative matters concerning foreign counterintelligence, including espionage, overseas homicide, protection of foreign officials and guests, domestic security, and nuclear extortion. It also coordinates the Security Countermeasures Program, which includes background investigations of personnel and physical security issues.

The Training Division, located in Quantico, Virginia, is where the FBI Academy trains FBI Special Agents and professional support staff, as well as local, state, federal, and international law enforcement personnel. Like any organization, the FBI depends on the caliber of its personnel, and staff receive training throughout their career, not just when newly recruited. There is also an Executive Training program for Chief Executive Officers, and an Operational Assistance Program, which trains law enforcement personnel to respond to certain emergency situations.

Central Intelligence Agency

The primary mission of the Central Intelligence Agency, or CIA, is to gather, assess, and circulate foreign intelligence in order to assist the president and senior U.S. government policy-makers in making decisions relating to national security. The Central Intelligence Agency does not itself make policy, but instead provides an objective source of foreign intelligence information that policy-makers may make use of in their decision-making. The CIA are, then, the eyes and ears of the government.

A History of the CIA

The CIA was formed under President Harry S. Truman in 1946 as an outcome of the events of World War II. Truman recognized that some kind of centralized intelligence agency was as necessary during peacetime as it was during war. Former New York lawyer and Major General William J. Donovan proposed a powerful, centralized civilian agency that would have authority to conduct "subversive operations abroad," but "no police or law enforcement functions, either at home or abroad."

The 1947 Act that created the CIA charged the agency with coordinating the nations intelligence activities and correlating, evaluating, and disseminating intelligence that might affect national security. Today, the Central Intelligence Agency is led by the Director of Central Intelligence (DCI), who manages the CIA in addition to serving as head of the entire U.S. intelligence community. The CIA works closely with the other organizations in the intelligence community and collects foreign intelligence information through a variety of overt and covert means, both at home and abroad. It serves as an independent source of analysis and works closely with other organizations in the intelligence community to ensure that policy-makers and battlefield commanders get access to the best intelligence possible.

Since the 1940s, the CIA has involved itself in foreign policy operations. In overseas situations, the CIA acts on behalf of U.S. foreign policy. For example, the CIA may **collude** in order to overthrow or block the actions of dictators. During the 1960s, at the height of the Cold War, the CIA was primarily focused on reducing and disabling the spread of Communist regimes.

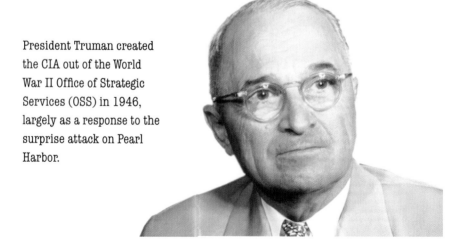

President Truman created the CIA out of the World War II Office of Strategic Services (OSS) in 1946, largely as a response to the surprise attack on Pearl Harbor.

Anti-Castro forces study a map in a tropical training camp prior to the attempted CIA-sponsored invasion of Cuba in 1961. The operation was an embarrassing failure.

The Bay of Pigs

The Bay of Pigs in Cuba is one of the CIA's best-known paramilitary operations of this kind. During the 1950s, President Eisenhower and Vice President Richard Nixon set up a CIA-run program to train hundreds of anti-Castro Cuban refugees in guerrilla combat in an attempt to overthrow the Castro government. The administration of President Kennedy, who was also worried by the Communist threat, decided to go ahead with this ambitious plan, although Senate Foreign Relations Chairman William Fulbright strongly opposed the proposed invasion.

The CIA planned a guerrilla landing in the Bay of Pigs in Cuba led by Cuban émigré pilots flying in American B26s disguised to resemble Cuban Air Force planes. When the invasion force landed at the Bay of Pigs on April 15, 1961, it met with more resistance than was anticipated and was quashed by Castro's forces, which took more than 1,100 prisoners during the fighting. The failure of this operation caused the CIA enormous embarrassment throughout the world.

The Cuban Missile Crisis of October 1962 followed, precipitated by the CIA discovery in Cuba of Soviet-made nuclear missiles capable of reaching most of the United States. This alarming discovery was made using human intelligence (HUMINT) and photographic intelligence (PHOTINT), and marked a turning point in the history of the National Security Agency and the CIA's overseas intelligence role.

At the height of the Cuban Missile Crisis, aerial photography was used to provide evidence of military installations perceived as threatening to the interests of U.S. national security.

The CIA and FBI have increasingly become involved in the global war on drug trafficking. Here, an antinarcotics agent patrols a jungle in Colombia.

The CIA produced detailed photographic intelligence identifying Soviet nuclear missile installations under construction on the island of Cuba, only 90 miles (145 km) off the Florida coast. At this point, President John F. Kennedy was forced to act. Facing the very real prospect of nuclear war, he chose to avoid invasion, and instead initiated a naval blockade against Soviet ships carrying missile equipment to the island. The Soviets withdrew the missiles, and nuclear war was averted.

The Creation of the Modern CIA

As the Cold War waned and the 1970s progressed, the CIA came increasingly under fire for its overseas role. In 1975, Senator Frank Church of Idaho headed the Senate Select Committee on Intelligence (later known as the Church Committee), which issued a report entitled "Alleged Assassination Plots Involving Foreign Leaders." This report claimed that the CIA was involved in assassination plots against Fidel Castro of Cuba, Patrice Lumumba of the Congo, and Ngo Din Diem of South Vietnam. The CIA was shown to have provided arms to various overseas **dissident** groups, and Executive Order 12333 of the 1981 Central Intelligence Agency explicitly limited the CIA from engaging, either directly or indirectly, in assassinations.

In 1984, however, President Reagan signed the Central Intelligence Agency Information Act, allowing the CIA to be excluded from the search- and-review requirements of the Freedom of Information Act. This freedom was granted in respect to operational and other sensitive files and granted the CIA a considerable degree of secrecy.

The CIA has emerged today as an independent agency, responsible to the president through the Directorate of Central Intelligence, or DCI, and accountable to the American people through the intelligence oversight committees of the U.S. Congress. Both the Congress and the executive branch oversee the Central Intelligence Agency's activities, which engages in covert action only at the presidents specific direction. The CIA specializes in addressing high-priority issues, such as nonproliferation of weapons and harmful substances, counterterrorism, counterintelligence, international organized crime, narcotics trafficking, environment, and arms-control intelligence. In order to achieve success in these activities, the CIA forges strong partnerships with the intelligence communities within the United States and throughout the world. CIA headquarters are at McLean, formerly known as Langley, in Virginia.

The CIA's declared mission has two main branches in order to support the president: the National Security Council, and all officials who make and execute U.S. national security policy. First, the CIA provides accurate, comprehensive, and timely foreign intelligence on national security topics.

Second, it conducts counterintelligence activities, special activities, and other functions related to foreign intelligence and national security as directed by the president.

The Mission of the CIA

By law, the CIA is specifically not permitted to spy on or gather information about U.S. citizens. Its mission is to collect information related to foreign intelligence and foreign counterintelligence. The CIA is only allowed to collect intelligence information on a U.S. citizen for an authorized intelligence purpose—for example, if there is a reason to believe that an individual is involved in espionage or international terrorist activities. Today, following the attacks on the Pentagon and the World Trade Center, the CIA works side-by-side with the FBI to prevent further threats to U.S. national security.

The CIA has three directorates, which are also known as special offices. They are the:

- **Directorate of Operations (DO)**

Headed by the Deputy Director for Operations (DUO), DO is primarily responsible for the covert collection of foreign intelligence, including HUMINT (human intelligence, or the use of human agents). Domestically, the DO collects foreign intelligence from individuals and organizations in the United States and is assisted by an Associate Deputy Director for Military Affairs (ADDO/MA).

- **Directorate of Science and Technology (DS&T)**

The Directorate of Science and Technology is headed by the Deputy Director for Science and Technology and provides support to the CIA and the intelligence community in the collection, processing, and exploitation of intelligence from all sources. These sources include imagery, HUMINT (human intelligence), SIGINT (signals intelligence), and other forms of intelligence data collected by clandestine technical means. The National Photographic Interpretation Center (NPIC) is also managed within the DS&T. NPIC is a joint CIA/Defense Department center and produces imagery-interpretation reports, briefing boards, videotapes for national-level consumers, and support for the military.

- **Directorate of Intelligence**

The CIA has worldwide scope, and its function ranges from immediate briefings on rapidly changing situations to long-term research studies that can take years to complete. The Deputy Director for Intelligence heads the Directorate of Intelligence (DI). The DI operates 13 different offices, including the CIA Crime and Narcotics Center, the Counterintelligence Center Analysis Group, and several regional intelligence centers, including one specifically on Iraq

CIA personnel officers may face extreme danger in the field—and sometimes pay with their lives. Johnny Michael Spann, whose casket is seen here draped in the U.S. flag, was killed in a violent prison uprising in Afghanistan in November 2001.

Selling National Secrets

During the 1980s and 1990s, three major cases of U.S. citizens spying against the United States were brought to light. Three men were major players in these cases. U.S. Navy Warrant Officer John Anthony Walker (pictured, left) sold top-secret encryption codes to the Soviets. Aldrich Ames, a 52-year-old long-time CIA employee attached to the Directorate of Operations (the CIA office handling global clandestine operations), was found to be a Soviet spy. Ames later acknowledged that as of May 1, 1989, he had been paid more $1.8 million by the KGB and that a further $900,000 had been set aside for him. Jonathan Pollard, a Navy intelligence analyst, leaked closely held secrets to Israel.

Text-Dependent Questions

1. Name some U.S. intelligence agencies.
2. What is the CIA's mission?
3. What does the FBI do?

Research Projects

1. Why does the United States have so many intelligence agencies? How well do these agencies work together?
2. Research the origins of the CIA. How does that relate to the way it operates today?
3. Has the CIA ever assassinated or tried to assassinate anyone?
4. Research Abu Graib. What can you learn about CIA interrogation techniques? Is torture ever justified?

The S.A.S counter-terrorist soldier

Binoculars

The Heckler and Koch Personal Defence Weapon

Weapon has "red hot "laser sights to project small but powerful beam along line of fire.

S.A.S "multiple bang stun grenades

P.E.4

Plastic explosive PE4, electronic detonator and detonating cord

BRITISH INTELLIGENCE AGENCIES

Words to Understand

Cipher: system for concealing text, either by switching the letters or numbers or by substituting other letters or numbers

Commonwealth: political organization consisting of nations loyal to the British monarch

Liaison: one who establishes and maintains communication for establishing and maintaining mutual understanding and cooperation

BRITISH INTELLIGENCE AGENCIES ARE LONG-TIME COLLABORATORS WITH THE UNITED STATES INTELLIGENCE AGENCIES. IN FACT, THE CIA IS LARGELY MODELED AFTER THE CENTRALIZED BRITISH EXAMPLE. BRITISH INTELLIGENCE SPECIALIZES IN SIGNALS INTELLIGENCE, AND THE MAIN SIGINT-GATHERING SITE IN THE WORLD IS GOVERNMENT COMMUNICATIONS HEADQUARTERS (GCHQ) IN CHELTENHAM, IN ENGLAND. THE BRITISH INTELLIGENCE COMMUNITY IS ALSO EXPERT IN COUNTERING TERRORIST ACTIVITIES, EXPERIENCE

The British special forces are well equipped to fight terrorism.

BASED ON A HISTORY OF MORE THAN 20 YEARS OF TERRORIST STRIKES BY IRISH TERRORIST GROUPS OPPOSED TO NORTHERN IRELAND'S CONTINUING MEMBERSHIP OF THE UNITED KINGDOM.

Organizations in British Intelligence

The British intelligence community has three main agencies, collectively known as "The Agencies." The Security Service, known as MI5, reports to the Home Secretary and is responsible for internal security, including counterespionage and antiterrorism. The Secret Intelligence Service (SIS) is also known as MI6. It is responsible for external covert operations, managing foreign agents, and covert gathering of information. Government Communications Headquarters is itself an agency, situated in a location that is an ideal world center for the gathering and de-encryption of SIGINT, or signal code. GCHQ works on behalf of Great Britain and other world intelligence agencies.

There are other agencies whose workings are crucial to British intelligence. The MOD (Ministry of Defence) runs the Defence Intelligence Staff (DIS), with agents distributed throughout British embassies worldwide, working to assess military capabilities and threat levels overseas. British Special Air Services (SAS) is a world-class paramilitary organization working against terrorists and reporting into the chain of command of the Ministry of Defense (MOD). The SAS is responsible for training most elite antiterrorist agencies around the world.

In the United Kingdom, intelligence gathering and analysis is governed by the Prime Minister, the Foreign and **Commonwealth** Secretary, the Home Secretary, the Defence Secretary, and the Secretary of the Cabinet. The main advisory body that determines priorities for intelligence gathering is the Joint Intelligence Committee (JIC), which is part of the Cabinet Office and reports to the Secretary of the Cabinet. The JIC coordinates the agencies in accordance with the priorities it sets and scrutinizes the performance of each agency. It also maintains a **liaison** with intelligence agencies in allied countries and aims to share information in the global community for the benefit of promoting a shared perception. The main groups that gather data or deploy intelligence in military activities are the Royal Air Force, the Royal Army, the Royal Navy, the Royal Marines, and the Royal Corps of Signals.

The three agencies collect intelligence and assist in government decision-making processes. The British intelligence community also contributes to longer-term analysis and produces regular reports that contribute to a comprehensive picture of global activities.

The Security Service: MI5

MI5 stemmed from the Secret Service Bureau and was expanded to meet the requirements of countering German espionage during World War II. Today, it is based at Thames House in London and reports to the Home Secretary. Since the Security Service Act of 1996, it has increased its responsibilities to provide support to law enforcement agencies fighting serious crime, such as drug trafficking. The Security Service provides domestic-security intelligence for Britain and is primarily responsible for protecting the nation from covertly organized threats, such as terrorism, espionage, and the proliferation of weapons of mass destruction. The main functions of MI5 are the interception of communications, eavesdropping (which involves covertly monitoring the speech of targets under investigation), surveillance (following and observing), and placing agents within target organizations. The Security Service submits its analysis of the various threats that menace the United Kingdom on an annual basis to an interdepartmental government committee. The government then puts security objectives in order of importance based on this report.

For four decades, the movie character James Bond has been how we imagine a British secret agent. Here, Pierce Brosnan plays Bond in the movie *Tomorrow Never Dies*.

The Secret Intelligence Service: MI6

Known as MI6, the Secret Intelligence Service evolved from the overseas department of the Secret Service Bureau that was responsible for gathering information overseas. MI6 was extremely significant during the Cold War and trained many famous spies. Today, it operates as part of the Department of the Foreign and Commonwealth Secretary, to whom it is directly responsible. It is regulated by the Joint Intelligence Committee, as is MI5. MI6's broad objective is to protect the interests of the United Kingdom in a global context and to counter foreign espionage and any perceived security threats.

MI6 is based at 85 Albert Embankment, Vauxhall Cross, in London.

MI6's main training center is Fort Monckton, on the south coast at Gosport in Hampshire. Trainees receive small-arms training at Fort Monkton, but much of the training is taken up with mastering advanced computer systems, encryption, **cipher** and communications work, and writing reports in the Secret Service style. The SIS (MI6) Technical Security Department is based in Oxfordshire. Stations abroad for MI6 are classified, from the high-risk Category A, such as the former Yugoslavia and Algeria, to the lesser Category B, such as Washington, D.C. and New York. Category C includes the countries of Europe, and Category D includes the Commonwealth, where there is little or no threat. Recently, MI6 has been boosting its presence in Southeast Asia and in China.

Government Communications Headquarters (GCHQ)

GCHQ is a civil service department under the responsibility of the Secretary of State for Foreign and Commonwealth Affairs. The Government Communications Headquarters dates back to World War I, but is better known for its decryption work during World War II at the most sophisticated centers for Signals Intelligence and Information Security research and application. GCHQ runs interception operations from the Cheltenham site and collaborates with a number of foreign intelligence and security services. It reports to the Government Joint Intelligence Committee, and its activities are governed by the approval of Cabinet ministers. GCHQ also advises on the national security of government and armed forces communication systems to ensure that sensitive information is properly protected.

The MI6 headquarters at Vauxhall Cross on the Thames River in central London, where Great Britain's secret intelligence service is based.

Defence Intelligence Staff (DIS)

Defence Intelligence Staff (DIS) forms part of the Ministry of Defence (MoD). It supports the Ministry of Defence, the armed forces, and other government departments by analyzing information from covert and overt sources and providing intelligence assessments, advice, and strategic warnings to the Joint Intelligence Committee, the MoD, military commands, and deployed forces.

The DIS manages two other agencies: the Defence Geographic and Imagery Intelligence Agency (DGIA), and the Defence Intelligence and Security Centre (DISC), responsible for providing imagery, geographic products, and intelligence training. The CDI, or Chief of Defence Intelligence, is responsible for the overall coordination of intelligence throughout the armed forces and service commands.

The Enigma machine was used to encipher and decipher messages. It had a keyboard and a lampboard, and each letter typed would be scrambled by the machine, and then light up the lampboard–always as a different letter. It was this scrambled message that was transmitted.

The Metropolitan Police

The Metropolitan Police first came into existence in 1829, when Sir Robert Peel was Home Secretary of Britain. Its headquarters were originally on a street in London, which was the former residence of the kings of Scotland, a site known as Scotland Yard. When these headquarters moved in 1890 to a site on the Victoria Embankment in London, they became known as New Scotland Yard. Today, the headquarters are in southwest London and are still known as New Scotland Yard.

The Metropolitan Police Service (MPS) plays an important role in countering terrorist attacks targeted at cities in England and Northern Ireland by Irish terrorist groups, including the Irish Republican Army (IRA) and the Real IRA. It is also responsible for safeguarding the security of members and ex-members of government, the diplomatic community, and the royal palaces. It is more than simply a metropolitan police force, in that it has high-tech communication links with the Security Service and is expert in anticipating and dealing with terrorist strikes. The MPS has a Directorate of Intelligence specializing in imagery and DNA testing. It is also expert in tracing suspicious financing and in covert surveillance.

The Special Branch of the Metropolitan Police was developed to counter terrorist activities during the movement for Irish independence. Special Branch is the most expert wing of the MPS in terms of countering terrorist attacks and has a long history of protecting the United Kingdom's capital from bomb threats and explosions originating from the activities of the terrorist groups the IRA and the Real IRA.

All agencies operate in secret, but are accountable to the Intelligence and Security Committee (ISC), which operates within a "ring of secrecy" to regulate expenditure, administration, and policy. The committee reports to the Prime Minister once a year.

The Echelon Program

Echelon is the world's most powerful intelligence-gathering network, a global communications interpretative system that links computers worldwide. Echelon can eavesdrop on more than three billion telephone, fax, and Internet communications around the globe every day. Western allied countries in the European Union developed it to protect their intelligence from being intercepted by Eastern-bloc countries. It was first established by the UKUSA alliance, a pact between five English-speaking countries made in 1947 between the United States, the United Kingdom, New Zealand, Australia, and Canada. Although the costs are shared, the United States National Security Agency provides most of the equipment and staffing.

As an interpretive system, Echelon differs from other such systems in two important ways. It can carry out virtually total surveillance using satellite receiver stations and spy satellites, and it can intercept almost any telephone, fax, Internet, or e-mail message. In addition, it is the only such system that is operated by security agencies of five countries.

The most controversial aspect of Echelon is that it operates free of legislation. Roaming across territories, it can eavesdrop on almost anyone in the world. In the late 1990s, claims were made that Echelon was being used for industrial espionage purposes, rather than for reasons of defense and national security.

Most intelligence agencies attempt to intercept foreign military and diplomatic communications, and may monitor civilian communications, too. Yet most democracies forbid intelligence agencies to spy on their own citizens. Human-rights groups, such as the American Civil Liberties Union and the Electronic Privacy Information Center, have called for a reevaluation of the information-gathering powers of Echelon.

The work of ECHELON, Five Eyes, and the NSA was brought to the world's attention in 2013, when former CIA employee Edward Snowden leaked a huge amount of classified information from NSA computers. It turned out that the NSA had been monitoring communications from millions of people, including government officials in other countries. It had also spied on online gamers by creating fictitious users, and had tracked the online sexual activity of certain people of interest. The NSA claimed that this was part of global surveillance and necessary in the war on terrorism, but many people were horrified to discover that the organization might have been syping on them. Snowden's leaks raised questions about privacy and cybersecurity and left the world divided in opinion; some called for restrictions on NSA spying activities and called Snowden a hero, while others labelled him a traitor for potentially sabotaging American intelligence efforts. Snowden himself was charged with theft of government property and violating the Espionage Act. He fled to Russia and applied for asylum, though by 2015 it had not been granted.

People protest government surveillance brought to light by whistleblower and former CIA employee Edward Snowden.

Text-Dependent Questions

1. What are the main British intelligence agencies?
2. Who governs intelligence gathering in the United Kingdom?
3. What does MI5 do?

Research Projects

1. James Bond is a fictitious British secret agent. What is the job of a secret agent really like? What do they do most days?
2. What role did MI6 play during World War II?
3. Look at the Secret Intelligence Service careers page. What MI6 job would you most like to do?

CHAPTER 6

FRENCH AND GERMAN INTELLIGENCE AGENCIES

Words to Understand

Militaristic: favoring a strong military and military-style government
Trafficking: dealing in illegal goods
Undercover: secret and concealed, disguising one's identity

IN FRANCE, THE DIRECTION GENERALE DE LA SECURITE EXTERIEURE (GENERAL DIRECTORATE FOR EXTERNAL SECURITY)Y WHO REPORTS TO THE MINISTRY OF THE DEFENSE, IS RESPONSIBLE FOR MILITARY INTELLIGENCE, STRATEGIC INFORMATION, ELECTRONIC INTELLIGENCE, AND COUNTERESPIONAGE.

During Algerian uprisings against the French colonizers, rioting took place and the French Army engaged in an all-out security hunt requiring militarized intelligence efforts. Here, a soldier checks the identity of all men and women passing through a checkpoint.

The DGSE has its origins in the External Documentation and Counterespionage Service (SDECE), which was formed from French intelligence after World War II and played an important role in the North African former French colony of Algeria. SDECE played a crucial role in controlling colonial French Indochina's illicit drug **trafficking** during the 1950s, when the Hmong poppy fields of Laos were linked with the opium dens operating in Saigon. During the 1960s, the SDECE was primarily involved with countering the rebellion in Algeria. In 1962, the SDECE was subordinated to the Ministry of the Defense and adapted itself to a military environment. During the 1970s, French Communists called for the dissolution of the SDECE. On April 4, 1982, the Directorate of the External Security (DGSE) replaced the SDECE. The DGSE was no longer permitted to operate on French territory, and the "militarization" of the DGSE was reduced. Today, civilians primarily operate the organization.

A poppy harvest in Laos. During the 1950s, illegal drug trafficking in the French Indochinese colonies became a major priority for French intelligence. Even today, the region known as the "Golden Triangle" (an area that incorporates part of Laos, Myanmar, and Thailand) is one of the world's biggest producers of raw opium.

Structure of the DGSE

- The Strategic Directorate maintains contact with the Foreign Ministry and suggests possible French political options.
- The Intelligence Directorate collects and distributes information, primarily from human sources, and is oriented to military intelligence, but is increasingly concerned with political, economic, and technological intelligence.
- The Technical Division is responsible for strategic electronic intelligence, and operates a number of listening stations throughout the world. The DGSE's main listening station is in the former French colony of Djibouti, North Africa.
- The Operations Division is responsible for planning and implementing clandestine operations. In the 1980s and 1990s, it implemented operations against the environmentalist group Greenpeace, and on July 10, 1985, DGSE agents detonated a bomb on the Greenpeace ship *The Rainbow Warrior* (pictured below) while it was in the port of Auckland, New Zealand, killing the photographer, Fernando Peira.

During World War II, the French organized to resist the Nazi occupiers of their country, laying the foundations for the modern-day DST.

The *Direction de la Surveillance du Territoire* (Directorate of Territorial Security), or DST, was created in 1944 as part of the effort to block invasion by Nazi Germany Since the 1970s, the DST has undertaken espionage activities in the military sector, as well as in economic, scientific, and technical areas. It is charged with the task of keeping abreast of all developments within and forms of global terrorism, and is administered as an internal security agency. Its mission is to trace all patterns of the threat, however uncertain or vague. The organization is subdivided into five subdirectorates (counterespionage, safety and protection of the patrimony, international terrorism, technical administration, and general administration), and has a special office of national and international relationships. It has four posts installed in overseas territories. The DST Economic Security and Protection of National Assets Department serves to protect French technology.

German Intelligence Agencies

The main tool of the National Socialists, or Nazis, in Germany was the SS, a specialized and **militaristic** government apparatus that took control over those territories that had come under German domination. The GESTAPO (*Geheime Staatspolizei*, or state secret police), founded in 1933, was the political police force of the Reich. It was one of the primary agencies for the persecution of the Jews, which ended in mass murder.

After World War II, Germany was split into democratic West Germany and totalitarian Communist East Germany. A secret police force, *Ministerium fur Staatssicherheit* (Ministry for State Security), also known as the Stasi, was established in April 1950 to prevent East Germans from collaborating with Western enemies and to monitor and control public and private activities in East Germany The Stasi had a network of informants to spy on almost all East Germans, so that the movements, loyalties, and political persuasions of anyone could be traced and exploited. Along with the Soviet secret police (the KGB), the Stasi spied on Western occupational forces in Berlin, NATO forces in West Germany, the West German government, and military and political bodies of the United States and other Western European countries. In 1990, West and East Germany were reunited, and the Stasi was dissolved.

Germany as a whole is renowned for its comprehensive and meticulous intelligence work. Today, the main intelligence agency is the BND, which reports to the Parliamentary Control Commission (PKK) for the intelligence services. The BND has operatives in more than 100 countries. Many agents work **undercover**, disguised as embassy staff members, as is typical of many intelligence agency workers throughout the world.

The BND is primarily concerned with the illegal trade in weapons and drugs, plutonium smuggling, armament or terrorist organizations, and threats to international traffic routes. It regularly transcribes telephone and radio conversations and telex and fax traffic. Today, the BND focuses on anti-American Islamic terrorist cells operating in Germany, and it is increasingly deploying Islamic activists to infiltrate such groups. The smuggling of nuclear materials and plutonium from former Soviet-bloc countries and Central Europe is another perennial area of concern, and the BND has an agreement with Russian intelligence agencies to cooperate in the area of contending with nuclear contraband.

The Federal Intelligence Service (BND) is headquartered in Munich-Pullach, where between 80 and 90 percent of BND employees are stationed. The BND operates a secret telecommunications intercept station in Hoefen at the border with Belgium.

Federal Office for the Protection of the Constitution (*Bundesamtes Für Verfassungsschutz*)

Called the BfV, this agency collects information about anticonstitutional activities in order to safeguard German democracy. It also investigates the activities of all foreign agents working in Germany on behalf of other intelligence agencies and closely scrutinizes any organization that might be considered a threat to national security. The BfV also engages in counterespionage. It reports to the federal and state governments, executive authorities, and courts and is accountable to the Federal Ministry of the Interior. The BfV gains the largest part of its information from open, generally accessible sources, including printed materials, such as newspapers, leaflcts, programs, and manifestos. However, in surveying such literature and media, the BfV watches for signs of any form of organized terrorism, from foreign terrorist cells operating on German soil, to homegrown Marxist or far-right antiestablishment activities.

Military Security Service
(*Militaerischer Abschirmdienst*)

MAD is responsible for military counterintelligence and is part of the main military offices of the German armed forces. Its main tasks are the collection and analysis of information about anticonstitutional efforts and adversary secret service activities, the interpretation of information for the assessment of the security situation of Germany and allied armed forces, and providing security evaluations and technical safety precautions for the protection of classified material.

The Federal Office for Information Technology Security (*Bundesamt Für Sicherheit in der in Formationstechnik*), known as the BSI, is a federal authority, created in 1990 and subordinated to the Federal Minister of the Interior. It is responsible for information technology security, including the processing or transmission of information.

Former head of espionage in Communist East Germany, Markus Wolf—nicknamed "The Man Without a Face"—came out publicly in 1989 with a book deploring the system for which he had formerly worked.

Text-Dependent Questions

1. What is the French intelligence agency?
2. What is the German intelligence agency?
3. Where is the German BND headquartered?

Research Projects

1. What are the main French intelligence operations today?
2. How do the German intelligence agencies spend their time and energy?
3. European nations are increasingly troubled by racial and ethnic conflict. How do European intelligence agencies monitor these activities and attempt to prevent terrorist attacks?

CHAPTER 7

ISRAELI INTELLIGENCE

Words to Understand

Anti-Semitism: hostility toward the Jewish people

Double agent: a spy pretending to serve one government while actually serving another

Infiltrate: enter covertly and undetected

MOSSAD, WHICH IS THE HEBREW WORD FOR "INSTITUTE," IS THE HIGHLY COVERT ISRAELI INTELLIGENCE SERVICE, PRIMARILY FOCUSED ON THE ACTIVE AND ACUTE PALESTINIAN TERRORIST THREAT, AND ON ANY POTENTIAL SIEGE BY ENEMY ARAB NATIONS. FORMERLY KNOWN AS THE CENTRAL INSTITUTE FOR COORDINATION AND THE CENTRAL INSTITUTE FOR INTELLIGENCE AND SECURITY, MOSSAD WAS FORMED ON APRIL 1, 1951. IT IS RESPONSIBLE FOR GATHERING INFORMATION AND COUNTERESPIONAGE, AND HAS MANY AGENTS WORKING IN FORMER COMMUNIST COUNTRIES ON BEHALF OF PERSECUTED JEWISH REFUGEES THERE. THE HEADQUARTERS OF MOSSAD ARE IN TEL AVIV.

Israel has been vulnerable ever since its conception as a new Jewish state on May 14, 1948, and has long required intensive intelligence and security operations. Here, Prime Minister Ben Gurion is seen at the moment of proclaiming statehood.

The History and Structure of Mossad

Due to Israel's history as a vulnerable conflict zone, Mossad has evolved since the 1950s to become one of the most militaristic intelligence agencies in the world. For Israel, security is a top priority, and the country depends heavily on the daring of its **double agents** working across Arab borders. Israeli intelligence is famous for infiltrating Arab states. Celebrated Israeli spies include Eli Cohen, who **infiltrated** the Syrian government before being discovered and publicly hanged in Damascus Square, and Wolfgang Lotz, who obtained crucial military information from Egyptian military and police officers in Cairo, including details of an Egyptian rocket program. As well as defending current Israeli national interests throughout the world, Mossad is also focused on the legacy of the Jews as a persecuted and displaced people. In 1960, Mossad kidnapped the Nazi war criminal Adolph Eichmann from Argentina, and in 1986, Mossad kidnapped the nuclear technician and Israeli traitor Mordechai Vanunu. Mossad also helps Jews in former Soviet-bloc countries to escape **anti-Semitic** communities and immigrate to Israel.

Israeli intelligence has been highly successful in tracing and putting on trial former Nazi officers responsible for the mass extermination of six million Jews during World War II. Here former Nazi SS Officer Adolph Eichmann stands behind bullet-proof glass in the Israeli Supreme Court in 1962.

Although most of its operations are highly covert, Mossad has eight known departments:

- The Collections Department is the largest department, responsible for espionage operations. It has agents working abroad covertly or under diplomatic cover.
- The Political Action and Liaison Department is the liaison authority that works in cooperation with friendly foreign intelligence services and with nations that may not have diplomatic relations with Israel.
- The Special Operations Division, also known as Metsada, is the top-secret assassination, sabotage, paramilitary, and psychological-warfare projects operations department.
- The LAP (*Lohamah Psichlogit*) Department is responsible for psychological warfare, propaganda, and deception operations.
- The Research Department gathers and produces intelligence information, including daily situation reports, weekly summaries, and detailed monthly reports. It has 15 geographically specialized "desks" spread throughout most of the world.
- The Technology Department recruits electronics engineers and computer scientists for the Mossad technology unit and is devoted to improving technological advantages and intelligence communications.

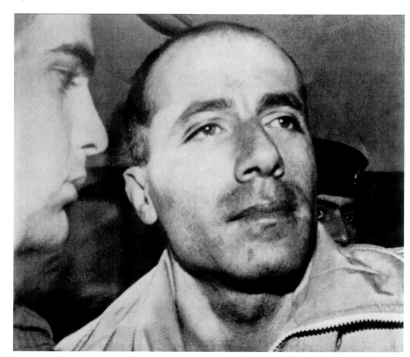

On September 30, 1986, Mossad captured and abducted whistleblower Mordechai Vanunu after he had leaked to the world top-secret evidence that Israel had become a nuclear power. Charged with espionage and treason, he was sentenced to 18 years' solitary confinement.

A young Palestinian boy throws a stone in the occupied West Bank in Palestine. Israel's long history of conflict means that Mossad, the nation's intelligence agency, is not afraid to take direct action against its enemies, including assassination attempts.

Defending the State of Israel

Unlike most other intelligence agencies, Mossad is overtly militant in nature. It is primarily involved with eliminating the Arab threat to Israelis and preventing murders and suicide bomb attacks by Palestinian freedom-fighting groups, such as the Palestinian Liberation Organization and Hamas. In pursuit of this, it has often taken direct action, which it has not sought to deny. During the 1970s, Mossad assassinated several Arabs connected with the anti-Israeli Black September terrorist group, and in 1988, it murdered PLO leader Yassir Arafat's deputy, Abu Jihad. Mossad also eliminated Gerald Bull, a Canadian scientist who developed the famed "Super Gun" for Iraq in March 1990.

It is not surprising that Arab states and international human-rights groups often criticize Mossad for the vehemence of its actions and for its extreme belligerence, which has resulted in some fatal mistakes. One of Mossad's most notorious actions took place on January 7, 1974. During an operation in Lillehammer, Norway, Mossad agents mistakenly killed an innocent Algerian waiter, Ahmad Boushiki, after they mistook him for the famous PLO security commander, Ali Ahmad Salameh. In response to this attack, the Norwegian authorities arrested the Mossad agents responsible and put them on trial before a Norwegian court.

More recently, Mossad suffered another severe blow, taking criticism for failing to prevent the assassination of Prime Minister Yitzak Rabin (by Israeli citizen Yigal Amir) on November 15, 1995. Mossad agents also failed in their attempt to assassinate Khalid Meshaal, a top political leader of the Palestinian group Hamas. On September 24, 1997, they entered Jordan on fake Canadian passports and injected him with poison. As a result of this attack, Jordan was able to negotiate the release of the founder of Hamas, Shaykh Ahmad Yasin, from an Israeli jail.

Regardless of such past failures, Mossad continues to play an essential part in maintaining Israel's security. Without it, the security of its people would be even more drastically at risk.

Other Israeli Intelligence Agencies

Shin Bet is the short form for *Sherut ha-Bitachon ha-Klali*, the general security service. Shin Bet is the Israeli counterintelligence and internal security service that monitors the activities of domestic right-wing fringe groups and subversive leftist movements. It works mainly by means of infiltrated agents and is particularly focused on immigrants and foreign visitors. Shin Bet gained a reputation for lying and false testimony in the 1980s to cover up fatal beatings and torture. Israeli authorities maintain that torture is not condoned, but acknowledge that human-rights abuses sometimes occur, although the results of investigations of such abuses are not made public. Shin Bet is divided into the following departments:

- The Arab Affairs Department is responsible for antiterrorist undercover operations, political subversion, and maintenance of an index on Arab terrorists.
- The Non-Arab Affairs Department is focused on all non-Arab countries and is responsible for penetrating foreign intelligence services and diplomatic

missions in Israel and interrogating immigrants from the former Soviet Union and Eastern Europe.

- The Protective Security Department is responsible for protecting Israeli government buildings and embassies, defense industries, scientific installations, industrial plants, and the El Al national airline.

Aman, short for Agaf ha-Modi'in, provides Israel with military intelligence for the prime minister and his Cabinet and conducts agent operations across borders. It is an independent service with a Foreign Relations Department, which is responsible for liaison with foreign intelligence services. It also has a department called Sayeret Maktal, the General Staff Deep-Reconnaissance Unit, which forms Israels primary counterterrorism and intelligence-gathering entity. Aerial reconnaissance and radio interception are used to gather information on Arab air forces. Remote-controlled drone aircraft are used extensively to observe enemy installations. Naval intelligence monitors naval activities in the Mediterranean and undertakes coastal studies in preparation for naval gunfire missions and beach assaults.

A protest on the Lebanon-Israel border by Hezbollah against Israeli attacks on Palestinians in the West Bank. Israeli intelligence agents are expert at gathering information in neighboring Arab countries and have infiltrated many Arab organizations in the interest of national security.

Center for Political Research, Ministry of Foreign Affairs

The Ministry of Foreign Affairs maintains diplomatic relations with 160 countries and works to protect the rights of Israeli citizens abroad. The Center for Political Research has 10 departments to monitor political developments, and focuses on gathering, analyzing, and evaluating political information. With expertise in Middle East affairs, it also helps the political information network, both in Israel and overseas.

Text-Dependent Questions

1. What is the Israeli intelligence agency?
2. What are some of Israel's security concerns?
3. What is Metsada?.

Research Projects

1. Investigate Mossad's efforts to find and arrest Nazis in the decades after World War II.
2. Mossad reportedly considered killing the Ayatollah Khomeini back in 1979. Read the book *Peripher: Israel's Serach for Middle East Allies* and find out more about this story and other Israeli security activities in the late 20th and early 21st centuries.
3. What does Shin Bet do? It has been accused of torture; are these accusations accurate?

SERIES GLOSSARY

Amnesty: pardon given by a country to citizens who have committed crimes

Anarchist: a person who wants to do away with organized society and government

Antiglobalization: against large companies or economies spreading into other nations

Appeal: referral of a case to a higher court for review

Arraignment: a formal court hearing at which the prisoner is asked whether he or she pleads "guilty" or "not guilty" to the charge or charges

Bifurcated: divided into two branches or parts

Bioassay: chemical analysis of biological samples

Biometrics: use of physical characteristics, such as fingerprints and voice, to identify users

Certificate of certiorari: a document that a losing party files with the Supreme Court, asking the Supreme Court to review the decision of a lower court; it includes a list of the parties, a statement of the facts of the case, and arguments as to why the court should grant the writ

Circumstantial evidence: evidence that can contribute to the conviction of an accused person but that is not considered sufficient without eyewitness or forensic evidence

Civil disobedience: refusing, in a peaceful way, to obey a government policy or law

Clemency: an act of leniency or mercy, especially to moderate the severity of punishment due

Commute: to change a penalty to another one less severe

Cryptology: the science and art of making and breaking codes and ciphers

Dactylography: the original name for the taking and analysis of fingerprints

Deputy: a person appointed as a substitute with power to act

Dissident: someone who disagrees with an established religious or political system, organization, or belief

Distributed Denial of Service (DDOS) attack: a malware attack that floods all the bandwidth of a system or server, causing the system to be unable to service real business

Effigy: a model or dummy of someone

Electronic tagging: the attaching of an electronic device to a criminal after he or she has been released, in order to track the person to ensure that he or she does not commit a crime again

Ethics: the discipline dealing with what is good and bad and with moral duty and obligation

Euthanasia: the act of killing or permitting the death of hopelessly sick or injured individuals in a relatively painless way for reasons of mercy

Exhume: to dig up a corpse, usually for examination

Exoneration: a finding that a person is not in fact guilty of the crime for which he or she has been accused

Extortion: the act of obtaining money from a person by force, intimidation, or undue or illegal power

Forensics: the scientific analysis and review of the physical and medical evidence of a crime

Garrote: to strangle someone using a thin wire with handles at either end

Gibbet: an upright post with a projecting arm for hanging the bodies of executed criminals as a warning

Graft: the acquisition of gain (as money) in dishonest or questionable ways

Grievance: a real or imagined wrong, for which there are thought to be reasonable grounds for complaint

Heresy: religious convictions contrary to church dogma and that deviate from orthodox belief

Hulk: a ship used as a prison

Hypostasis: the migration of blood to the lowest parts of a dead body, caused by the effect of gravity

Incendiary: a bomb

Infiltrate: to enter or become established in gradually or unobtrusively, usually for subversive purposes

Intern (v.): to confine or impound, especially during a war

Interpol: an association of national police forces that promotes cooperation and mutual assistance in apprehending international criminals and criminals who flee abroad to avoid justice

Intrusion detection system (IDS): software designed to detect misuse of a system

Junta: a group of military officers who hold power, usually as the result of a coup

Jurisprudence: a system or body of law

Ladder: an early form of the rack in which the victim was tied to a vertical framework and weights were attached to his ankles

Lag: a convict

Latent: present and capable of becoming obvious, or active, even though not currently visible

Lockstep: a mode of marching in step where people move one after another as closely as possible

Lynch: to attack and kill a person, typically by hanging, without involvement of the courts or legal system and often done by a mob

Manifesto: a written statement declaring publicly the intentions, motives, or views of its issuer

Manslaughter: the unlawful killing of a human being without express or implied intent

Martyrdom: the suffering of death on account of adherence to a cause and especially to one's religious faith

Mercenary: a man or woman who is paid by a foreign government or organization to fight in its service

Miscreant: one who behaves criminally or viciously

Molotov cocktail: an explosive weapon; each "cocktail" is a bottle filled with gasoline and wrapped in a rag or plugged with a wick, then ignited and thrown

Money laundering: to transfer illegally obtained money through an outside party to conceal the true source

Mule: a person who smuggles drugs inside his or her body

Mutinous: to resist lawful authority

Paramilitary: of, relating to, being, or characteristic of a force formed on a military pattern, especially as a potential auxiliary military force

Pathologist: a physician who specializes in examining tissue samples and fluids to diagnose diseases

PCR: polymerase chain reaction, a technique of making multiple copies of a small section of DNA so that it can be analyzed and identified

Personal alarm: a small electronic device that a person can carry and activate if he or she feels threatened

Phreaker: a person who hacks telephone systems

Pillory: a device formerly used for publicly punishing offenders consisting of a wooden frame with holes in which the head and hands can be locked

Political asylum: permitting foreigners to settle in your country to escape danger in another country, usually his or her native land

Postmortem: an autopsy; an examination of a dead body, looking for causes of death

Precedent: something done or said that serves as an example or rule to authorize or justify a subsequent act of similar kind

Pyramid scheme: an investment swindle in which some early investors are paid off with money put up by later ones in order to encourage more and bigger risks; also called a Ponzi scheme

Quick: the living flesh beneath the fingernails

Racketeering: the act of conducting a fraudulent scheme or activity

Ratchet: a mechanism consisting of a "pawl," a hinged catch that slips into sloping teeth of a cogwheel, so that it can be turned only in one direction

Repatriation: returning a person to his or her country of origin

Ruse: a subterfuge in order to distract someone's attention

Screw: slang term for a prison guard

Scuttle: to cut a hole through the bottom, deck, or side of a ship

Seditious: of, relating to, or tending toward an incitement of resistance to or insurrection against lawful authority

Serology: the laboratory analysis of blood serum, particularly in the detection of blood groups and antibodies

Siege (n.): a standoff situation, in which a group holds a position by force and refuses to surrender

Slander: a false and defamatory oral statement about a person

Smash and grab: a term used to describe a method of stealing, where thieves break windows (for example, on a shop front or a car) to grab the goods within before fleeing

Statute: a law enacted by the legislative branch of a government

Statutory: authorized by the statute that defines the law

Subversive: characterized by systematic attempts to overthrow or undermine a government or political system by persons working secretly from within

Succinylcholine: a synthetic drug that paralyzes muscle fiber

Vendetta: an often-prolonged series of retaliatory, vengeful, or hostile acts or exchange of such acts

White-collar crime: crime committed by office staff, usually involving theft from the company they work for

Worm: a computer program that enters one computer and replicates itself to spread to other computers; unlike a virus, it does not have to attach itself to other files

Xenophobic: having an unreasonable fear of what is foreign and especially of people of foreign origin

CHRONOLOGY

1939–1945:   During Word War II, British codebreakers, using "Colossus," crack the German "Enigma" code; U.S. intelligence cracks Japanese codes and begins the "Venona" program to decipher encrypted Soviet diplomatic communications.

1946:   March, Cold War begins.

1947:   Congress passes the National Security Act that establishes the National Security Council (NSC) and the CIA.

1956:   J. Edgar Hoover launches COINTELPRO, targeting antiwar demonstrators, pacifists, antinuclear activists, and civil rights leaders with wiretapping, eavesdropping, and threats.

1960:   The NSA begins intercepting messages revealing a Soviet military buildup in Cuba.

1961:   April, Central Intelligence Agency-backed invasion of Cuba at the Bay of Pigs fails; Director of the CIA, Allen Dulles, is forced to resign; the Berlin Wall is erected between West and East Berlin.

1962:   October, U.S. intelligence reconnaissance discovers Soviet missiles in Cuba; the United States blockades Cuba for 13 days until the Soviet Union agrees to remove its missiles.

1965–1975:   Vietnam War features heavy CIA involvement and FBI monitor of antiwar activities at home in the United States.

1971:   British expel 105 Soviet intelligence officers due to Cold War tensions.

1975–1976:   Congressional "Church Committee" investigations reveal that United States government agencies, including the NSA, eavesdropped and spied on U.S. citizens involved in civil rights and anti-Vietnam War movements; in response, the House and Senate create permanent committees to regulate the U.S. intelligence community; William Colby, Director of the CIA, testifies that the CIA was engaged in coups and attempted assassinations abroad, was spying on U.S. citizens, and was conducting controversial drug and mind-control experiments; he is forced to resign.

1978:	Congress passes the Foreign Intelligence Surveillance Act to regulate electronic intelligence gathering.
1984:	President Ronald Reagan issues a directive giving the NSA responsibility for maintaining the security of government computers.
1985:	Naval Soviet spy John Walker is arrested.
1986:	Dmitri Polyakov, USSR double agent betrayed by CIA mole Aldrich Ames, is assasinated.
1989:	The Berlin Wall is torn down; many Communist governments in Eastern Europe collapse; after German reunification, Markus Wolf, head of East Germany's spy agency from 1958–1987, is charged with espionage, bribery, and treason and sent to prison.
1991:	Gulf War reveals weaknesses in United States intelligence and spurs new military-intelligence advances.
1994:	Aldrich Ames, a KGB mole inside the CIA, is convicted and sentenced to life in prison without parole.
1998:	NSA "Echelon" controversy arises; a European Parliament report states that the project targets civilian communications and political advocacy groups.
1999:	November 5, White House national security advisor advises the United States to recognize its dependence on information systems for intelligence purposes.
2001:	Robert Hanssen, an FBI agent, is arrested for spying for the Soviet Union/Russia; September 11, the attack on the World Trade Center and the Pentagon by terrorist group Al Qaeda leads to a subsequent tightening of global security and a recruitment drive by the U.S. intelligence community in an effort to increase counterterrorism efficiency.
2013:	Former CIA employee Edward Snowden leaks vast amount of classified material collected by global surveillance programs held by the National Security Agency, revealing that the NSA was tracking millions of emails and messages around the world.

FURTHER INFORMATION

Useful Web Sites

Central Intelligence Agency (CIA): www.cia.gov

Eutelsat: www.eutelsat.com

Federal Bureau of Investigation (FBI): www.fbi.gov

UK Government Communications Headquarters (GHCQ): http://www.gchq
.gov.uk

INTELSAT: www.intelsat.com

National Security Agency (NSA/CSS): www.nsa.gov

Secret Intelligence Service (MI6): www.sis.gov.uk

Further Reading

Alpher, Yossi. *Periphery: Israel's Search for Middle East Allies.* Rowman &
Littlefield, 2015.

Andrews, Christopher, et. al. *The Sword and The Shield: The Mitrokhin
Archive and the Secret History of the KGB.* New York: Basic Books, 2000.

Andrews, Christopher. *For the President's Eyes Only: Secret Intelligence and
the American Presidency from Washington to Bush.* London: Harper
Collins, 1995.

Bamford, James. *The Puzzle Palace: A Report on America's Most Secret
Agency.* London: Penguin, 1983.

Dennis, Mike. *The Stasi and East Germany: 1950–1990.* London: Longman,
2002.

Dulles, Allen. *Craft of Intelligence: America's Legendary Spy Master on the
Fundamentals of Intelligence Gathering for a Free World.* Lyons Press,
2006.

Hennessy, Peter. *The Secret State: Whitehall and the Cold War.* London: Allen
Lane, The Penguin Press, 2002.

Hiro, Dilip. *Sharing the Promised Land: An Interwoven Tale of Israelis and Palestinians.* London: Hodder & Stoughton, 1996.

Kerby, Phil. *With Honor and Purpose: An Ex-FBI Investigator Reports from the Front Line of Crime.* New York: St. Martin's Press, 1998.

Lowenthal, Mark. *Intelligence: From Secrets to Policy.* CQ Press, 2014.

Morell, Michael. *The Great War of Our Time: The CIA's Fight Against Terrorism, from al Qa'ida to ISIS.* Twelve, 2015.

Porch, Douglas. *The French Secret Services.* Basingstoke: Macmillan, 1996.

About the Author

Joanna Rabiger was born in London, England, and was educated at Cambridge University and Columbia College, Chicago. She has worked for the London-based publishers Cassell and The Womens' Press, and in the editorial division of the trade books department at Oxford University Press. In 1999, she moved to the United States to train as a film editor at Columbia College, Chicago, concentrating on documentary work. She now works as a freelance writer and documentary film editor in Austin, Texas. While a film student in Chicago, Joanna also worked as a researcher for the Emmy award-winning documentary production company Nomadic Pictures. For Nomadic, she contributed developmental production work on a TV series on women public defenders and the U.S. criminal justice system, and researched the role of prison ministries and support systems for recently released prisoners, covering such topics as race, incarcerated parents and their children, drug rehabilitation, halfway houses, employment issues, and re-offending.

INDEX

PICTURE CREDITS